the cool
lunchbox

sandy harper

I dedicate this book to my mother, whose passion for food lit a candle in my heart.

I miss you very much, and wish you were here to share this with me!

the cool
lunchbox

NEW
HOLLAND

Acknowledgements

Over the years I have found much inspiration in books and magazines and to the authors of these I owe a huge debt of gratitude. More importantly, however, I need to thank all my friends who encouraged and supported me in this particular venture. Of course, I am also especially grateful to my wonderful family, who never doubted me for an instant. I could not have done this without your love and ongoing support. And, to my two daughters, Megan and Lauren, who were on the receiving end of my experiments, thank you so much. Your sense of humour and refreshing honesty is what kept me in line!

Finally, my thanks go to Magdaleen van Wyk for her technical support and guidance – I am truly indebted to you.

SANDY HARPER

The author and publishers wish to thank the following outlets for their kind assistance and the loan of props for the photography: Cape Union Mart, Hotchiwitchu, Lim, Loads of Living, Nocturnal Affair, Plush Bazaar and The Yellow Door.

First published in the UK in 2004 by New Holland Publishers (UK) Ltd
London • Cape Town • Sydney • Auckland
www.newhollandpublishers.com

Garfield House, 86–88 Edgware Road, London W2 2EA
80 McKenzie Street, Cape Town 8001, South Africa
14 Aquatic Drive, Frenchs Forest, NSW 2086, Australia
218 Lake Road, Northcote, Auckland, New Zealand

Copyright © in published edition: Struik Publishers 2004
Copyright © in text: Sandy Harper 2004
Copyright © in photographs: Images of Africa 2004

Reproduction by Hirt & Carter Cape (Pty) Ltd
Printed and bound by Sing Cheong Printing Company Limited

PUBLISHING MANAGER: Linda de Villiers
EDITORS: Sean Fraser and Joy Clack
DESIGNER: Beverley Dodd
PHOTOGRAPHER: Lucinda Mudge/Hirt & Carter
STYLIST: Abigail Donnelly

10 9 8 7 6 5 4 3 2 1

ISBN 1 84537 003 1

Contents

Introduction

How many times have you been confronted by a lunchbox that needs to be filled, and wondered what on earth to put into it? Or, worse still, one that comes back and has hardly been touched? Most children leave home early in the morning and only return in the afternoon, so the majority of their nutritional needs must be met by the contents of their lunchbox. And what about your own nutritional needs? Do you rely on a packed lunch to sustain you for the day?

Packed lunches aren't a new concept. They have been around for centuries – when men and women went out to work in the fields, a billycan or other suitable container was filled with the previous night's leftovers, and tied securely with a napkin to keep the food warm. Those days may be long gone, but the need for packed lunches has remained. For children of all ages, a packed lunch is commonplace, with many having to pack extra food for the afternoon's sporting activities.

More and more working adults also rely on a packed lunch for their lunchtime nutritional requirements, rather than use their short lunch breaks to queue in a canteen or buy something from the 'sandwich lady'.

Preparing a packed lunch or lunchbox needn't be a drudge. In fact, with a little creativity, the packed lunch can become the highlight of the day. If you approach it as if you are packing for a picnic, the task of preparation will be more fun and certainly a lot more rewarding.

For most youngsters, eating isn't the social occasion their parents and other adults have come to enjoy. In fact, for most children, eating is something that needs to happen quickly and efficiently so that no valuable time is lost, which could be devoted to doing the things they would rather be doing, such as playing. So, with this in mind, the contents of children's lunchboxes should:

- be designed to have **visual appeal,** in order to entice children to eat;
- be **as simple as possible,** so that it can be eaten in the shortest possible time;
- include items that encourage **repeat visits to the lunchbox** during the course of the day;
- include **easily digestible foods** – lunches are often eaten in haste and not chewed properly.

At the same time, the contents of the lunchbox must provide the necessary nutrients to sustain children's busy schedules! So, how can you achieve this?

This book has been designed around the needs of children of school-going age, as well as adults who take their lunch with them to the workplace. The same basic principles and recipes can be used for any age group; only the quantities need to be adjusted to make them age appropriate.

Most people have neither the time nor the inclination to create complicated 'menus' from detailed recipes, so most of the lunch suggestions in this book focus on the combination of flavours rather than on the meticulously measured quantities of ingredients. The recipes that I have included are extremely simple and have worked well for my family over the years. Many are also great as a substitute for conventional breakfasts – those often drawn out rituals that we either can't bear to face so early in the morning or simply have no time to prepare or sit through.

Love in a lunchbox

My husband and I and our two daughters were out walking in the mountains one fresh morning – nothing too hectic, just a gentle walk that quickened my heart rate slightly but still allowed me to take in the beauty of my surroundings and to observe my two bunnies running along the path with more energy than I care to remember myself ever having. Seeing them so free, I couldn't help but ponder this role I have, the one we call motherhood. And then, as if reading my thoughts, my husband turned to me and asked, 'What legacy will we leave our kids one day?'

We walked on in silence, each caught up in our own thoughts. Reaching our favourite tea-time spot at the waterfall, we sat down to enjoy some refreshment while we watched the girls paddling in the icy water. I hadn't thought about an 'outcomes-based' approach until then. I had just done the best I could as each day presented itself to me – coping with each event as it came. Now I was asked to think about what I would like the girls to have as a living memory of me during this journey called life. And then it came to me...

I want them to be equipped to make informed decisions in life. And, perhaps because my life-long passion and interest is firmly rooted in food, I especially want to empower them to make the right choices with regard to food. Whether we like it or not, we are what we eat, and the food we consume affects us in so many ways. So many children have suffered as a result of lifestyle and food habits that stem from uninformed decisions.

Many teenage eating disorders can be traced to the ways in which they were introduced to food and eating, and formed habits, which over time created the blueprint of how they would conduct their lives as adolescents and adults.

I believe that one of the most important 'legacies' we can leave our children is to teach them to appreciate good, healthy food, and to make the right choices to ensure optimum health. We, as parents, are instrumental in shaping the relationship our children develop with food, and if we don't maximize this opportunity, the fast-food culture in which we live – aided and abetted by glamorous advertising – will do it for us!

The suggestions and easy-to-follow menus and ideas in this book have been specifically created as time-savers. To say that our lifestyle today is busy is a gross understatement of the frenetic pace at which we live our lives. With so little time to spend with family, we need to develop new ways of using the time we do have if quality family life is still to be enjoyed. Chatting to your children about healthy eating habits and engaging them in the discussion around their lunchbox is a sure way of opening up the channels of communication regarding food in general. Why you include certain ingredients in the lunchbox is a great way for them to learn about nutrition and to appreciate the care and love that goes into that box. All items in the lunchbox need to be age appropriate, but even little ones will find it exciting to discover what mum has packed for snack time.

Food can be a very powerful medium through which you can communicate with your children. The love and attention with which you package each meal communicates to your children all the wholesome values of caring, nurturing, thoughtfulness and understanding so often lost in the race against time that is our lives.

What this book's about

See this book as your own DIY manual for packed lunches and lunchboxes. The boxes are varied and each has been carefully planned to include all the right sorts of goodies to make the snack interesting, tasty, nutritious and generally appealing. The lunchboxes are quick and easy to put together, simple yet nutritious, using basic ingredients available in most households, and should also stimulate your own ideas about what would work for your children. There are over 40 lunchbox menus, plus suggestions on sandwich fillings and a list of protein and carbohydrate snack options from which to choose. The idea is to mix and match the lunchbox items to suit your child's own needs and preferences. Play around, and have fun experimenting. I have also included basic nutritional facts so that you may understand more fully why certain items pop up regularly in these menus.

My aim with this book is to lighten the burden of parents who face the seemingly never-ending cycle of lunchboxes day after day, week after week, and to provide some new inspiration for their own packed lunches.

introduction

How to use this book

As I mentioned previously, this is not a conventional recipe book, although I have included a handful in the last chapter. It has been designed to be an easy reference guide, which you can dip into without having to read the entire book.

However, to get the full advantage of what I am trying to achieve, I urge you to read this book from cover to cover in order to gain a working knowledge of what I mean by 'balance'.

The tips and 'Did you knows?' have been included to impart bite-sized bits of information to empower you to adapt each meal to suit your needs.

If you or anyone in your family is prone to allergies or intolerances, it is best to read the section on pages 33–34 before you start packing the lunchbox. Other than in the case of severe allergies, I am a firm believer of not excluding ingredients entirely from the diet but rather to moderate the intake of 'offending' products.

I have tried to stick to ingredients that are commonly found in most households. These are not new, but hopefully their application in this book will inspire you to package them in exciting and different ways.

the
basics

Get real!

As a teenager, there were times I thought that I knew all the answers. But I will never forget the day my dad opened his huge atlas to a double-page spread of the solar system that showed the sun in the foreground and the various planets around it. Somewhere, in the dark distance, was a tiny pinprick, which Dad pointed out as earth. His words to me were that I should imagine how small earth is in the context of the solar system, and a fraction of it is a continent called Africa. At the tip of this great land mass is a country called South Africa. And somewhere in South Africa was a little girl who thought she knew all the answers!

I think my journey with food has taught me that we really *don't* have all the answers. The human race is constantly evolving, and so too is the food that we eat and how we react to it. The 'information age' is slowly burying us in all the information regarding the food we should eat. Many advertisements will have us believe that food producers have all the answers. And amid the bombardment of advice on what we should eat, when, where, with whom and with which napery, people are making their own choices regarding their eating habits – habits that will shape their lives forever.

So, I believe that when things get a little fuzzy, we should get back to the basics!

However unsexy they may seem, the basics are precisely what we have all lost sight of. And the most important principle of getting back to basics is balance – that delicate state where all things work in harmony. I believe that we should all simplify our lives and strive to regain a balance. And the best way to start, is with food.

This book isn't about radical ideas, New Age methodologies or nutritional philosophies. It's about balance... It's about being practical... And it's about having fundamental information to hand so that you are empowered to make informed decisions about your health and that of your children.

Bear with me as we take another look at some of the old basics. It's on these fundamental principles that this book has been based, and understanding and appreciating them will make the contents more useful and the composition of the various lunchbox menus will make more sense.

Protein, carbohydrates and fats

Protein

Protein, which provides the basic building block of the human body, is made up of amino acids. These amino acids are the main source of building material for our tissues, organs, hormones, enzymes and immune system. There are approximately 22 amino acids, most of which are called 'non-essential', as the body is able to manufacture these from other sources. But not all amino acids can be made by the body. Eight 'essential' amino acids have to be supplied through diet, and these are found in animal products such as meat, fish, poultry and dairy products as well as plant sources, which include nuts, beans, peas and soy products, such as soy flour, soy milk and tofu.

Unlike carbohydrates, protein requires a longer and more complicated process to break down to its fundamental building blocks in order to release its energy value. Thus protein must be included in the diet for growth and more sustainable energy.

Carbohydrates

Carbohydrates are plant based, and include all grains and starches, fruits and vegetables. Carbohydrates, however, are complicated foodstuffs, and the trick lies in striking a balance. Carbohydrates (stored in the body as glycogen) are the body's preferred source of energy. Glycogen breaks down to carbohydrate's most basic form, glucose, which the body calls upon for its energy. There are two types of carbohydrates: simple and complex.

Simple carbohydrates are those foods closest to their building-block form, and they therefore require little digestion in order to release energy. An example of these simple carbohydrates is fruits, but they also include sugar, which is best limited in the diet. The simple sugars (monosaccharides) found in fruits and vegetables provide the body with vitamins and minerals, small amounts of protein and plant fats, as well as dietary fibre. Fruit is an ideal way to inject instant energy in the diet.

the
basics

Coleslaw wrap *(Vegetarian lunchbox 5, page 43)*

Chicken salad with mango and pecan nuts *(page 61)*

Sausage and mustard roll *(page 64)*

Pasta salad (General lunchbox 2, page 36)

Complex carbohydrates, on the other hand, are broken down by the body at a much slower rate, and thus sustain blood-sugar levels for much longer. Examples include all grain products (preferably whole-grain), pulses, whole-wheat pasta, oat bran and whole-wheat breakfast cereals. Complex carbohydrates are a particularly important part of breakfast for school-going children, as they help kick-start the day, and should sustain them until snack time. In fact, it's for this reason that complex carbohydrates also form the foundation of children's lunchboxes.

Carbohydrates form a vital part of any meal and particularly snacks. They provide the bulk of the meal, but also offer the vitamins and minerals the body requires to perform at its peak.

Snacking on simple sugars in refined foods – a snack bar or soft drink, for example – might provide instant energy, but they are depleted very quickly and energy levels fall rapidly. As a result, there is the temptation to snack again, which becomes a vicious cycle. Snacking on complex carbohydrates won't, however, spike the blood sugar in this way, and thus will sustain you for much longer.

Fibre

Dietary fibre is found only in plant foods such as fruits, vegetables and whole grains. Most of us know about wheat fibre and the term 'wheat bran' or 'roughage', but many people aren't aware that there are two kinds of fibre.

First, there is *soluble fibre*, which is found in fruits and vegetables, legumes, barley and oats; and then there is *insoluble fibre*, which is found in wheat, brown rice and maize. Some vegetables also contain insoluble fibre.

Once again, it's important to have a good source of both kinds of fibre in the diet. Not only does it provide the necessary bulk in the diet to aid digestion, but studies have shown that a diet rich in fibre lowers blood-cholesterol levels, thus preventing diseases such as colon cancer and heart disease. All in all, a fibre-rich diet will improve overall health and wellbeing.

Sugar

The terms 'blood sugar' and 'blood-sugar levels' are popular buzz words today, but what is all the fuss about, and why is it so important to monitor the levels of sugar in the diet?

Blood-sugar blues

All the food we consume is ultimately broken down to the basic energy our bodies need to function. This energy is transported via the bloodstream to the cells, and is referred to as blood sugar. The key to optimum health is to keep the blood sugar at a constant level, thereby ensuring that sufficient energy is available at all times for all the bodily functions. Some of the foods we consume, such as refined sugar, are simple sugars and don't require much in the way of digestion to make them available in the bloodstream. These sugars are, however, unable to sustain this level of energy for a long time.

When a sudden surge of sugar enters the bloodstream, it shocks the pancreas into producing more insulin in order to cope with the additional glucose. The insulin effectively removes all the glucose from the blood, reducing the blood sugar content to a level below what it was before the sugar injection. This fluctuation, or 'spiking', of blood-sugar levels has been blamed for many behavioural problems, including irritability, aggression, lethargy, mood swings and even depression.

Hypoglycaemia is a severe form of low blood sugar, where blood-sugar levels drop to such a degree that you feel light-headed, weak and sometimes even nauseous.

The Glycaemic Index (GI) identifies foods according to their ability to release energy through the breakdown of complex sugars into their basic form, glucose. Generally, foods with a low GI score (in other words, below 50), are good for you, while foods with a score of 70 and above are best avoided or at least minimized. Intake of foods with a GI score of between 50 and 70 should be limited.

The best way to determine which foodstuffs are best in your diet, is to remember that complex carbohydrates release their sugar slowly into the bloodstream, thus providing energy over a longer period. If protein is added to the meal, the rate of release is slowed even more.

Sugar has also, however, long been associated with the destabilization of the blood-sugar levels and the subsequent depletion of Vitamin B stores in children and adults alike, resulting in hyperactivity or confusion and the inability to concentrate or focus.

Apart from the obvious problem of tooth decay, sugar has also been linked to a variety of other health issues, including nasal congestion, asthma, depression of the immune system and migraines. It can also interfere with the absorption of certain minerals, in particular calcium and magnesium, cause chromium deficiency in the body, stimulate the onset of thrush (*Candida albicans*) – and so the list goes on! Of course, it's also addictive and can become very difficult to avoid.

Refined sugar is hidden in a variety of foods, but should nevertheless be avoided – or intake at least minimized – wherever possible. In fact, the lunchbox should be one area where sugar is restricted to natural sugars. Avoid cakes and cookies, chocolate bars, doughnuts and similar sweet goodies. Stick to honey or natural preserves and jams and delete the refined sugar items from your shopping list. If you don't have them in the house, you can't pack them in the lunchbox!

Fruits also contain simple sugars called glucose and fructose, but these come packaged with all the vitamins and minerals you need – and in a form that is readily available to the body so they require little digestion before they enter the bloodstream.

Some fruits, such as grapes and dates, contain pure glucose and will be absorbed even faster into the bloodstream. Bananas, on the other hand, contain both fructose and glucose and, unlike pure glucose, isn't a rocket fuel that will spike your blood sugar and then fizzle out just as quickly. The sugar in bananas is readily available, making them ideal for raising sugar levels rapidly if necessary. Bananas, as with all fruit, come 'packaged' with fibre and small amounts of protein and fat, which all contribute to sustaining blood-sugar levels.

Fats

Fats come in all sorts of forms – truly a case of 'the good, the bad and the ugly'! *Good* fats are plant fats and carry fat-soluble vitamins and essential fatty acids, both of which perform vital roles in the body. These plant fats can be either monounsaturated or polyunsaturated fats, and can be found in avocados, sesame and other seeds, olives and olive oil, and in nuts, grains.

Bad, or saturated, fats are linked to many health problems and are found mostly in animal (including dairy) products and even in coconut milk. The *ugly* fats, on the other hand, are the excess fats that we consume and that can lead to heart disorders and obesity. Also remember, however, that too much fat – no matter what the source, be it good, bad or ugly – will lead to weight issues and even obesity. Again, we need to strike a balance. As a general rule of thumb, make sure that your fat consumption doesn't exceed 30 per cent of your daily food intake.

It's important to remember, however, that we do actually need fats and oils in our diet. They provide very important nutrients, but we need to monitor our intake of the quality of fat, not only the quantity.

Did you know?

The heating procedures some oils go through during processing cause the formation of free radicals that may be detrimental to your health. The body also doesn't have the enzymes to break down and digest fats that been heated to very high temperatures.

Water and the fruit juice frenzy

Our bodies comprise roughly 60 per cent water, but considering the volume of fruit juice we allow our children to consume, you would think our bodies were made up of fruit juice instead.

Check the credentials of your family's favourite juice and see if it's truly 'nothing but fruit'. On closer inspection, you will be amazed at just how few brands of juice are 100 per cent natural. Most have added sugar, many have preservatives, and a host of brands that call themselves 'juice' are actually a concentrate in disguise!

These 'fruit juices' have a very high sugar content, high acidity and none of the fibre benefits offered by whole fruit. Furthermore, most have been thoroughly processed, depleting them of their vitamin and mineral content – the very reason for eating fruit in the first place! In fact, unless the juice contains fruit pulp, you are only getting half the value for the same amount of kilojoules.

This high sugar content in fruit juice (as well as other artificial cooldrinks) isn't only detrimental to healthy blood-sugar levels, but also promotes tooth decay. This is particularly true of children who are given juice as infants. 'Juice babies' often lose their milk teeth far too early, paving the way for more serious dental problems later in life.

The excess sugar can also lead to weight problems if it isn't carefully monitored.

Why water?

Water is such a basic substance that we seem to have forgotten just what a wonderful nutrient it is. Water is the most essential component of blood and protoplasm, the fluid that helps our body cells function properly. It's the vehicle through which most of our essential bodily functions take place, from moistening the lungs for oxygen absorption and maintaining body temperature, to lubricating and protecting our joint surfaces and facilitating food digestion and absorption. Water also plays an integral part in the brain. Neurotransmitters rely on water in order to efficiently relay signals from cell to cell. So, if your child doesn't drink enough water, the brain could suffer from a mild form of dehydration, causing 'brain stress'. As the brain struggles to cope without adequate lubrication, children could simply 'switch off'. This form of dehydration could also exacerbate existing learning difficulties.

What we need to do is to reintroduce children to the habit of drinking water – either tap water or filtered or natural spring water. Whatever your choice, it's important to establish the principle of drinking water to quench a thirst. Other beverages may supplement a meal or be drunk as social drinks, but thirst should always be quenched with water first. In the lunchbox menus that follow, I suggest

the
basics

water as the first option. Eat the fruit and drink water! To make the water the delight that it should be, freeze the water bottle before placing it in the lunchbox. The ice will have melted by lunch time, but the water will still be cold and will have also kept the contents of the lunchbox cool – a sort of reusable ice brick. Or, if the water is going to be required sooner than lunch time, fill the water bottle to two-thirds full and freeze, then top it up with water at room temperature just before popping the bottle into the lunchbox. Establish a new trend, and just watch the other children start including water.

Learning difficulties and behavioural problems

A growing number of school-going children are being diagnosed with Attention Deficit Disorder (ADD) or Attention Deficit Hyperactivity Disorder (ADHD), and yet these are probably the most misunderstood and mismanaged 'illnesses' in our modern society.

According to Professor André Venter, Head of Paediatric and Child Health at the University of the Free State and South Africa's leading authority in learning disabilities, ADD and ADHD are caused by an imbalance of neurotransmitters (chemical messengers) in the brain. There may be many causes, but the most significant is genetics.

Having combed a number of books researching the role of nutrition in behavioural problems and learning difficulties, one thing stands true: while a healthy diet may not cure your child of ADD or ADHD, it will certainly assist him or her in dealing with the problem far better than a diet filled with excess refined sugar, additives and preservatives.

Having taken the step towards the nutritional option, finding your way around the supermarket becomes a nightmare. Grocery aisles are a minefield of sugars and additives, many of which will no doubt be your child's favourites. All the lunches in this book, however, comprise simple, basic ingredients and have been designed to keep your child's blood-sugar levels at a reasonably stable plateau throughout the day by providing a variety of nutrients that do just that.

The key here is to keep the blood sugar from plummeting, which – even in children who don't have ADD or ADHD – will leave a child lethargic, ill-tempered, weepy or moody, with an inability to focus and poor concentration. An even keel – that is what children need more than anything else. And, bearing in mind that each child is unique, it must be remembered that each child will respond differently to new diets and new lunchbox items.

Medical intervention

If your child is on medication such as Ritalin, his or her appetite may well be inhibited. It's no use packing the lunchbox with too much food; children will simply be overwhelmed by all the food and may be put off eating the few items that really matter. It will also dishearten you, especially when you have gone to all that trouble to prepare the lunchbox. Rather acknowledge the problem by discussing his or her lack of appetite with your child, explaining that you will pack the lunchbox with just a few healthy items that he or she will enjoy eating even if he or she isn't really hungry. In other words, reduce the quantity, not the quality.

The focus of this book is on sustaining children during the day, when they are reliant on a packed lunch for their nutritional needs. I do, however, need to emphasize that you need to make quite sure that they have the right breakfast to arm them for the day – and this is particularly true for children with special needs. I have included a few recipes for children who don't like to eat early in the morning. See, for example, my Yummy Breakfast Muesli on page 68, which is adaptable to cater for most allergies, aversions or general dietary restraints. It's quite delicious and may also be used to fill the gaps as an in-between snack. Do try to avoid those commercial 'box' cereals that are sugar-coated and filled with harmful preservatives as they tend to spike the blood sugar.

Invest the time to whip up a cooked breakfast; it doesn't take long. This doesn't always mean bacon and eggs; you could make a steaming pot of wholesome porridge, and remember, too, the benefits of oats. You will be well rewarded for making the necessary effort.

Try to include little nibbles that are more often associated with 'snacking' than with having a meal. Kids don't eat popcorn because they're hungry, but because it's associated with a fun activity like watching a movie. Use this psychology to pack the lunchbox. Add small portions of snacky things like popcorn or dried sausage sticks or biltong. Raw carrots and a small wedge of hard cheese or dried fruit are all 'disguised' foodstuffs that can be nibbled on, rather than approached as a whole meal.

These kids also tend to be ravenous when the medication wears off. Remember to have that wholesome meal ready in time, even if it means making your usual dinner time a little earlier.

There are some excellent books on how to cope with ADD and ADHD, and the Hyperactive and Attention Deficit Disorder Support Group of South Africa offers advice on understanding the demands placed upon you as parents, and may be able to direct you to a group in your own town or city. The Pretoria-based group can be contacted either by telephone (012) 997 0256/7, or via their website at www.adhdsupport.co.za. Or form your own support group and share your successes.

Obesity and portion sizes

The June 2003 edition of the popular American magazine, *American Way*, ran an article in which it stated that more than 60 per cent of American adults are overweight; of these, nearly half may be classified as obese. It stated further that almost one in two Americans will die of heart disease, making it the nation's number-one killer. While the magazine doesn't purport to be a scientific or medical journal, the statistics are nevertheless alarming. And the reason for this state of affairs? Quite simply, American children have never been taught how to eat properly! Of course, society is looking at all sorts of excuses, blaming everything from the fast-food culture, TV meals and the disappearance of family mealtimes, to nutritional teaching aids such as the old-fashioned food pyramid.

Unfortunately, however, children learn their eating habits from their parents – and the fast-paced lifestyle of Western society has meant that we have resorted to a fast-food culture. But the buck stops here!

How and *what* we teach our children about food has a direct bearing on their health as adults and their quality of life as they grow older. We can't simply expect them to 'do as I say, not what I do' and hope that the effects of lethargy will escape us. Children need to be taught about portion sizes and what is appropriate in terms of quantity. Less is indeed more; rather increase the quality of the snacks than the quantity. Children need to be taught to respect food and to understand why we eat in the first place. They need to develop a passion for good, healthy food, and not a dependency on junk food. Teach your children to love beautifully prepared food and to understand our interdependency on the earth for our food and preservation. It all, however, starts with our own commitment and the relationship we, as parents, have with food.

In some cultures, food is a status symbol, where being overweight is regarded as a sign of prosperity. My sister teaches at a school that draws huge numbers of rural children, most of whom arrive at school with half a loaf of bread and a litre of milk for snack time. In this instance, the volume of food is out of balance with the nutritional value it offers. During the year, my sister gently encourages her pupils to bring less food to school, but to vary the ingredients so as to ensure that they too learn about appropriate portion sizes and optimum health. We all share the responsibility to teach our children about good eating habits.

This book doesn't dictate portion sizes. This depends largely on the individual. The menus here also offer a variety of different ingredients that may be added to the total meal complement. Monitor your children, speak to them about their lunchbox contents. If, for example, you pack two sandwiches and one comes back, try sending one sandwich and increase the quantity of the support ingredients.

Let us build a healthy, lean nation. Start by teaching your children the difference between feeling hungry and a simple – 'M-o-m, I feel like…'. You will soon find the 'just right' amount for your kids. Wasting food should be regarded as a sin.

Cholesterol

For those of us who have heard all the hype about cholesterol, but can't quite remember all the facts, here they are in a nutshell…

The body has two sources of cholesterol: that which it manufactures itself, and that which is derived from what we eat. Sources of cholesterol include meat, fish, poultry, eggs, butter, lard and cream – in short, animal fats.

It's important to remember, however, that cholesterol performs vital functions in the body, including the production of sex hormones and bile acids, and also plays an important role in keeping body tissues healthy. Cholesterol is fat-soluble and thus needs a transporter to help it move through the bloodstream (which is water based). Low-density lipoprotein (LDL) transports the cholesterol from the liver, the prime manufacturer of cholesterol, to the cells, while high-density lipoprotein (HDL) transports it away from the cells and back to the liver for secretion. Hence, LDL is referred to as 'bad' cholesterol and HDL as 'good' cholesterol. The balance of cholesterol in the body is very important. Too little cholesterol has been associated with aggressive behaviour and even strokes, while too much leads to heart disease.

After the initial hype around cholesterol, most of us stopped eating butter and changed to margarine. Well, just to confuse everyone, recent research has indicated that simply cutting out animal fats may not be enough to avoid heart disease. The latest research indicates that a lack of nutrients in the diet, especially Vitamin C, has an even greater role to play, and that eating up to three eggs per week has

the
basics

no significant effect on blood cholesterol levels. But now that butter is back on the shopping list, it doesn't mean that excessive animal fats are permitted. The most recent reports confirm that we need a healthy, balanced diet filled with plenty of fresh raw fruits and vegetables. Use plant oils – where possible, olive oil – when cooking and in salads. Olive oil has the added advantage of lowering the level of LDL in the bloodstream. If you do suffer from high cholesterol, then stick to skinless chicken breasts or smoked chicken and remove all visible fat from cold-meat cuts such as ham, beef or lamb. More importantly, include raw vegetables and fruits, as well as whole grains in order to provide the necessary vitamins and minerals required in your diet. And if you are still not sure about your options, consult your doctor or a registered dietician.

All the vegetarian lunchboxes as well as the general lunchboxes and their vegetarian options given in this book, are cholesterol friendly. Adult lunch suggestions that are not suitable for cholesterol sufferers have been indicated.

Did you know?

Monounsaturated fat ('good' fat, if you are concerned about cholesterol) is found in olive oil, almonds, hazelnuts and avocados.

packing the
'power lunchbox'

Get creative!

Just as children adopt the cultural and religious influences of their parents, their eating habits and food preferences are based on what they experience at home. The wider your repertoire, the better chance you have to induce your child to try new flavours. Younger children usually have a limited spectrum of preferred items and are quite happy to have the same old favourites on a regular basis. The 'bland' approach is thus usually the 'safe' option when it comes to preschool children, but older children might be keen to experiment with stronger flavours and a more varied routine. Adults quickly get bored with the same food but, fortunately, the choices are as many and as varied as the imagination. I have included some wonderful new ideas; many may seem foreign to you, but try them out – they are truly delicious!

First impressions

The old saying, 'Never judge a book by its cover', certainly doesn't apply to food. First impressions are lasting, so we need to follow a few guidelines in packing a lunchbox. From a very early age, children learn to be discerning and will often refuse to even taste food that doesn't look appealing. The same principle applies to the lunchbox. It's therefore very important to change the 'look' of the contents even if the food items are all basically the same. What follows are a few hints on how to present the lunchbox so that it looks different every day.

- **Change the shape of the sandwich.** With all the different kinds of bread and rolls available from your local supermarket or deli, changing the 'look' of the sandwich isn't difficult to achieve. You could also slice the sandwich in different shapes – two rectangles one day, two triangles the next and four squares another, for example.

- **Change the shape of the rolls** by including long hotdog rolls, soft round rolls, round sesame rolls, oval cheese rolls and curved croissants. It all makes for a good first impression and a varied lunchbox – and is one step closer to an empty container! Rye breads and rolls can also be included to increase the variety.

- **Water is vital to a balanced diet.** Encourage your child to drink more water by including water rather than juice in your child's lunchbox.

- **Include a boxed juice on some days and decanted 'bottled' juice on others.** While the juice part of meal remains the same, the container varies and thus the perception of variation. In summer, juice (or water) can be frozen and put in the lunchbox in the morning. This will help keep the contents cool and fresh, and it will have thawed by snack time.

- If you always wrap the sandwiches in plastic, **try wrapping the sandwich in tinfoil or wax wrap** for a change. Your child will be intrigued to find out what surprises lie within the folds.

- **Include a small message on special days.** This could be a good way of building a special form of communication between you and your child.

- **Add a small pack or portion of a high-energy snack** such as nuts and raisins, dried fruit or home-made date balls (see page 70).

- **Try to prepare the lunchbox the night before.** Remember to wrap sandwiches individually in wax wrap and then in sandwich bags to retain flavour and freshness before placing them in an airtight container in the fridge.

- **An occasional treat shows that you have put some thought into the lunchbox** and will carry you for a few days if the contents have tended to be a little boring! These 'treats' should, however, still fall within the gambit of a healthy

packing the 'power lunchbox'

Pita bread filled with chicken,
apricots, parsley and lettuce
(General lunchbox 8, page 39)

Sandwich shapes with a variety of toppings *(page 28)*

Pita pocket filled with potato salad (*Sports lunchbox 2, page 49*)

Croissant with ham, cheese, lettuce and grainy mustard
(General lunchbox 3, page 37)

Lettuce wrap with smoked salmon *(page 65)*

Tammy's rusks *(page 68)*

Flapjacks with fresh plums, raspberries and honey *(page 58)*

Fruit kebabs *(page 59)*

snack. Try including freshly buttered spice buns (hot cross buns) or a banana muffin instead of a sandwich. A croissant with grated cheese and a thin spread of strawberry preserve may also be seen as a special treat.

All these suggestions will help make the first impression of the lunchbox one of surprise and delight, but the most important hint is changing the shape of the sandwich. By varying the bread forms, you are more than halfway there!

Creating variety

Get the balance right. The ideal lunchbox should contain the following:

- **Protein**.
- **Carbohydrate** (the bulk of the lunch, but make sure you include complex carbohydrates).
- **Fruit**.
- **Water and/or fruit juice**.
- The occasional **treat**.

Protein snacks

Protein provides the body with the same amount of energy as carbohydrates, but its main function in the diet is to build and repair cells. A small amount of protein in the meal will sustain blood-sugar levels for longer than a meal without protein. Below are some ideas for snacks that are high in protein.

- Mini chicken kebabs.
- Cold meat wrapped around a gherkin, or tinned asparagus or a finger of cheddar cheese.
- Chicken pies (a good sandwich alternative).
- Cold chipolata sausages.

- Cold boerewors or beef sausage sliced or left in 'finger' lengths and put in a separate container.
- Cold, crumbed chicken breasts sliced thinly and wrapped in tinfoil.
- Whole hard-boiled eggs.
- Mini meatballs (see page 71).
- Chicken drumsticks.
- Biltong (sticks or slices) and dried sausage.
- Nuts (preferably raw); include a variety, such as almonds, cashews and pecans, and not just boring old peanuts!
- Lentils and other pulses (these are great sources of plant protein).
- A variety of seeds, including sunflower, sesame and pumpkin seeds, which are all very good sources of plant protein. They also contain very important essential fatty acids and fibre.
- Greek-style yoghurt decanted into a smaller container with honey and nuts. The nuts, raisins, oat bran and other additions may also be placed in separate containers.

- Small, individual fruit-flavoured yoghurts.
- Individual cheese portions (there is now a great selection available) or, for younger children, you could cut cheese into shapes with a cookie cutter. Use the offcuts in lieu of grated cheese on sandwiches.

Carbohydrate snacks

The two carbohydrate groups – complex carbohydrates and simple carbohydrates – provide the bulk of the energy of the meal. Simple carbohydrates include all fruits and vegetables, so include some of the following in your lunchboxes:

- Baby tomatoes.
- Fresh vegetable fingers, including carrots, celery, baby corn, baby cucumbers, red and yellow peppers.
- Sprouts.
- Fruit in any form – fresh or dried or even in the form of natural juice.

Simple carbohydrates are packed full of vitamins and minerals that the body needs to perform all its functions.

Complex carbohydrates, on the other hand, include whole grains such as brown rice, rye, oats, whole-wheat bread, pasta and corn, which may be included in the lunchbox in different ways.

- Whole-wheat or rye sandwiches with various fillings.

- Whole-wheat breadsticks, with a small tub of chunky, low-fat cottage cheese mixed with chopped ham and gherkins.
- Pasta salad, comprising tuna or chicken, gherkins, cucumber, feta cheese and a little mayonnaise.
- Pasta salad with baby pork sausages, and roasted red and yellow peppers mixed with basil pesto.
- Brown rice salad (see page 53).
- Potatoes (baked whole or boiled baby potatoes or as potato salad), preferably with the skins on.

Refined carbohydrates, such as white flour and white bread, sugar, cakes and biscuits, should be limited in the diet and care should be taken to include whole grains or balance the meal with plenty of raw fruits and vegetables.

Did you know?

White flour is also a complex carbohydrate, but due to the refining process it goes through to achieve this white, fluffy product, much of the nutrient value is lost. As a result, white flour also contains negligible amounts of roughage.

The best way to sustain blood-sugar levels is by combining complex carbohydrates with small amounts of protein.

packing the
'power lunchbox'

Fruit

In her book, *The Natural Way*, Mary-Ann Shearer calls fruit 'the most perfect food', and describes it as 'the most complete food we can eat' because it's easy to digest, contains all the nutrients (vitamins, minerals, proteins and fats) we need, it is in an accessible form, and the simple sugars provide instant energy in the diet.

Fresh fruit should be included in a packed lunch whenever possible, and your choice will inevitably be dictated by your child's preferences. Try, however, to vary the standard inclusion of the banana or apple by packing a small container with sliced fruit such as kiwifruit, pear or watermelon, or seedless grapes or even dried-fruit options such as fruit rolls, whole dried fruit or fruit squares. Granadillas cut in two and held back together with an elastic band makes for a novel experience, but remember to include a spoon.

A small fruit salad could also be included. Fruit can also be sliced and placed on a small kebab, which makes it easier to handle and introduces visual appeal.

Water and/or fruit juice

Water remains the best option, and the role of fruit juice in our children's diet should be seen as supplementary to the meal. It shouldn't be seen as the thirst quencher. Try to find a juice that has no added sugar and no additives or preservatives. Some commercial juices use ascorbic acid (Vitamin C) as a natural preservative. There are many good juice options available, so find a brand that you can trust and stick with it.

Treats

Treats should be just that – treats. They shouldn't be included too often, as they will become everyday expectations. Try some of the following suggestions for occasional lunchbox surprises.

- Banana-and-nut or bran muffins.
- Buttered spice buns (or hot cross buns).
- Cocktail sausage rolls (if warmed in the morning and wrapped in tinfoil, they will still be warm by snack time).
- Small containers of sunflower seeds and pumpkin seeds or fresh berries – gooseberries, cherries and strawberries.
- Peanut-and-raisin clusters.
- Popcorn. Microwave popcorn allows you to prepare it fresh on the day. Place it in a sealed container or zipper-locked plastic bag or it will go soggy.
- Home-made bran rusks (see Tammy's rusks on page 68).
- Honeyed nut brittle (see page 70).
- Oat crunchies.
- Date balls (see page 70) and sun-dried figs and fresh dates.
- Cereal treats (without harmful preservatives).

packing the
'power lunchbox'

The sandwich

Research has shown that no matter what else you pack in a lunchbox, the most important item remains the *sandwich*. In whatever form that takes, it still provides the most effective snack food which, together with the filling, provides most of the energy requirements and the bulk necessary in the lunch-box. Other items, such as the fruit, provide the roughage and vitamin and mineral requirements.

With the wonderful assortment of different styles of bread and rolls available, the sandwich should never be boring. Alternate the choice of bread every day so that you make good use of the variety that is available. For working mothers and those who don't get to shop regularly for fresh bread, ready-to-bake rolls are the answer. Placed in a hot oven directly from the freezer, these rolls make fresh bread readily available to every household.

When you are caught short and there is no fresh bread in the house, you could also improvise by using crispbread products such as Pro-Vita®, Ry-Vita® or even rice cakes and the like.

Include whole-wheat breadsticks as an extra, interesting nibble. Cut large rolls in half. One half might only be eaten later in the day, and this way the remaining half remains presentable for fussy eaters. It also makes the rolls easier to handle and easier for smaller mouths to negotiate. Whole-wheat pita or pocket breads and whole-wheat muffins may also be included to add to the variety. As a rule, try to use whole-wheat bread products, but occasionally include other products such as croissants or cheese bagels just for a change. Too much whole-wheat might turn your child off it for life! And always remember that it's all about *balance*.

Cool fillings

- Thinly sliced, smoked chicken breast with cucumber, lettuce and mayonnaise.
- Spread avocado mixed with a little lemon juice on one slice of bread, and low-fat cottage cheese on another. When sandwiched together, they make an interesting colour combination!
- Experiment with the variety of cold meats now available at supermarkets and delis. Try different flavour combinations, such as mild chutney with roast beef or creamed horseradish instead of mayonnaise on a chicken or turkey roll.
- The addition of sliced gherkins to a cold-meat and lettuce sandwich gives it a lift.
- Bacon with cucumber and horseradish makes for a substantial filling.
- Chunky cottage cheese with toasted sunflower seeds, thinly sliced pineapple and a drizzle of honey.
- Finely grated biltong with low-fat cream cheese and cucumber.

- Crispy chopped bacon and peanut butter.
- Chunky or smooth cottage cheese mixed with a little freshly grated carrot and a few seedless sultanas. Raw carrots contain high levels of betacarotene (Vitamin A) necessary for healthy skin and eyes. Eaten raw, they also have a naturally cleansing effect on the bowels.
- Chopped boiled egg with mayonnaise. Try including freshly chopped parsley for taste and nutrition. Parsley is a great source of vitamins A and C and, because it's eaten raw, you get all the goodness it contains.
- Tinned tuna mixed with finely chopped tomato, avocado and mayonnaise.
- Use steamed or roasted butternut as a spread with chicken or avocado.

And don't forget the peanut butter, fish paste or vegetable and meat spreads such as Marmite® or Bovril®. These are great back-up spreads and can be regularly included in your repertoire.

Some children don't like sandwiches. To encourage them to eat their lunch, you could simply leave out the bread, and put some of the fillings suggested above in a small container and provide a spoon or fork. Crispbread or breadsticks may be used as a substitute for the traditional slices of bread.

Remember to wrap sandwiches with 'wet' fillings in wax wrap before placing them in their sandwich plastic. It's also a good idea to wrap each half of the sandwich individually. This will not only retain the shape and contain the filling, but will also keep the sandwich fresher for longer.

TIPS

If the filling comprises cottage cheese, avocado, mayonnaise or similar spreads, it isn't necessary to spread the bread with margarine or butter.

If you are prone to fungal infections, limit your intake (don't exclude it entirely) of bread and spreads such as Marmite, as the yeast content could aggravate the condition. Regularly include unleavened bread products, rice cakes, pancakes and other alternatives.

To create visual interest, cut the sliced bread into interesting shapes using cookie cutters.

cool
lunchboxes

Get organized:

When I was growing up, I always thought my mother had such a 'clever' cupboard and a 'clever' fridge! She could produce the most amazing snacks in no time at all if guests suddenly pitched up for a glass of wine, or afternoon tea drifted into sundowners. And, of course, she allowed us to help make the snacks, so our limited imaginations were all that kept us from putting Nigella Lawson out of business!

It was only years later that I realized that it wasn't the cupboard that was clever, it was my mum! My mum took 'being organized in the kitchen' to a another level. Here was a lady who had every item in her huge deepfreeze labelled with dates and shelf numbers, and as it was used she would tick it off and include it on the shopping list. She was awesome!

What she taught me is that life is a lot less stressful if you do a few simple things. There is no doubt that in order to avoid the lunchbox frenzy, get organized. It makes your life so much easier.

Start with dedicating a space in the pantry or grocery cupboard, or a separate drawer for snack items. Make sure you have a number of small containers of varying sizes, plastic spoons and/or forks and some colourful paper serviettes. The lunchbox container itself also requires some thought. Find one that will take all your child's snacking goodies without squashing the items, and is deep enough to fit in a few extra little containers for those little nibbles.

Once you have sorted out the 'tools of the trade', it's time to create a 'clever cupboard'. Try to stock a few of the items listed overleaf. Some may need to be stored in the fridge, so in no time you will too have a 'clever fridge'!

'Clever cupboard' contents

- **Containers**. Keep a variety of containers of different shapes and sizes.
- Lightweight **tinfoil**.
- **Wax wrap**.
- Perforated **clingfilm**.
- Reusable **zipper-locked plastic bags.**
- Large plastic **sandwich bags**.
- Colourful **paper serviettes**.
- Plastic **spoons, knives and forks.**
- **Breadsticks**. There are a variety on the market. Try to avoid the plain white ones and rather opt for the sesame or whole-wheat sticks.
- **Cheese straws**. Decadent, but one or two in a box are a great occasional treat.
- **Crispbreads**. There are many readily available brands of crispbreads, including Ry-Vita®, Pro-Vita® and other whole-wheat varieties. These are a great substitute when, on a Sunday night, you discover there is no fresh bread to make the lunchbox sandwiches.
- Ready-to-bake **rolls and breads** in the freezer.
- **Brown rice and pasta**. Choose pasta shapes that are easy to eat with a fork.
- **Nuts**. Keep a variety from which to choose, including almonds and red-skinned peanuts, which are a good source of fibre. Make a batch of honeyed nut brittle (see page 70) and store it in an airtight container.

- **Couscous and rice noodles**.
- **Condiments**. Stock a selection of grainy mustard, creamed horseradish, and fruit chutney. Also keep pesto sauces (basil pesto or sun-dried tomato pesto) in vacuum-sealed packs. These only require refrigeration after opening, and do wonders for a pasta salad.
- Tinned **tuna and salmon**.
- **Olives and extra-virgin olive oil**.
- **Herbs** from pots on the patio or from the garden.
- A selection of unprocessed **cheese wedges**. Alternatively, cut cheddar into small portions and wrap in wax wrap and clingfilm.
- **Fruit** products. Dried fruit, fruit rolls, raisins, currants – there is such a fun variety from which to choose, and they are great for the Sunday-night scramble.
- Once a week, stock up on **fresh fruits and vegetables** and, if appropriate, a selection of **cold meats, chicken cuts,** and so on.
- Develop a **'lunchbox mentality'**… Think of easy-to-eat items while doing the household shopping.

Develop a new way of looking at packed lunches. Experiment. Get the kids involved. Most importantly, have fun! Look out for different ideas in magazines, which often have plenty of new thoughts and presentations. Get organized. It will simplify your life.

Allergies and substitutions

A surprising number of adults and children suffer from some form of allergy or intolerance. There are far too many to cover here, so I have focused on the two most common intolerances, namely wheat intolerance and lactose (dairy) intolerance, and have also included a section on nut allergies.

Allergies are far more serious than intolerances, as they induce an instant reaction to a particular ingredient. People with allergies are mostly alert to what they can and can't eat, as it's usually quite easy to identify the offending food. Food intolerances are, however, more difficult to manage, as the 'symptoms' are often a number of 'built-up' reactions to a particular food.

If your child always seems to have a running nose, is slightly under the weather, has a poor appetite, is lethargic or develops skin irritations such as eczema, and all the obvious medical causes have been ruled out, have him or her checked for a wheat or lactose intolerance, the most common of childhood intolerances.

Learn to find alternatives (I have provided some) and make better use of other lunchbox items that your child can tolerate. If you arm yourself with a list of additional options, creating easy, tasty snacks for the packed lunch should never be a nightmare.

Be mindful of food fads. Make sure your exclusions are really health related rather than fashion driven.

Wheat intolerance

Wheat intolerance is usually caused by gluten, the protein substance in wheat. Items that contain smaller amounts of gluten or are completely gluten free are listed below. Remember: moderate rather than exclude. These foods may be used to substitute wheat products:

Cereals	Oats, muesli, polenta, maize meal, sorghum.
Breads	Rye bread and breads made from buckwheat flour, pumpernickel bread and breads such as naan bread and roti or burritos.
Pasta	Pasta made from corn, and rice noodles or buckwheat noodles.
Treats	Oat-meal crumpets, shortbread biscuits made from cornflour or wheat-free muffins.
Alternatives	Samp (dried maize kernels), rice, barley, sweetcorn, cornflour, potato flour, rye flour, buckwheat flour

> **Did you know?**
>
> Some people can't tolerate rye bread or even oats. Experiment with the lunchbox menu to determine to what extent your child may be intolerant of these.

Lactose (dairy) intolerance

Lactose is the sugar content in milk. Some people are allergic to cow's milk, or simply avoid dairy products because they tend to produce a build-up of mucus. However, I tend to be very sceptical about eliminating particular foods from the diet, as this is often prompted by fashion fads and not by real intolerance. It's simply a matter of balance. Every individual has his or her own level of tolerance for certain foods, including dairy. The problem may be no more than a slight build-up of mucus, so individuals should determine their own tolerance levels rather than eliminate dairy completely.

Cutting out dairy does mean that alternative sources of calcium and protein must be found. Here are a few alternatives if you are lactose intolerant:

Milk	Soya milk is the most common, but rice milk or oat milk is also available from most health shops.
Cheese	Tofu is a protein-rich curd made from soya beans.
Butter	Olive oil or margarine.
Calcium	Foods rich in calcium include nuts, especially almonds, hazelnuts and cashews. Dried fruit such as apricots, figs and peaches. Dark green vegetables such as broccoli, Brussels sprouts and dark-leafed vegetables such as spinach.

Did you know?

Some children who are intolerant of milk are able to enjoy yoghurt. This is because the lactose content in yoghurt is already partially converted, making it easier for children or adults, who would otherwise be lactose intolerant, to tolerate.

Butter is a far healthier product than we've been led to believe it to be. Most people – even children – can tolerate butter even if they can't tolerate milk.

Nut allergies

Nut allergies, once hardly heard of, have become much more prevalent and most manufacturers are required by law to state on their packaging whether prepared foods contain nuts or, in fact, if the item has been prepared in the same factory where nuts have been processed. This is a severe allergy and teachers and work colleagues should be made aware of it.

If you or your child suffers from an allergy to nuts, replace nut snacks with a suitable alternative, such as dried fruit.

General lunchbox menus

In the following section I have suggested various menus, which can be used as they are, or adapted to suit your child's food preferences, cultural beliefs and sensitivities. These menus are based on very simple ingredients that should appeal to children of all ages.

All these menus have been compiled on a mix-and-match basis. If there is an offending food in a menu, simply replace it with a suitable substitute from the suggestions on pages 25–27. The menus also follow the same basic composition and can be adapted according to preferences or availability.

I have also provided a vegetarian option for each lunchbox. The idea here isn't to be prescriptive, but to show how lunchboxes can vary, yet remain true to the principles set out previously. Further variety can be introduced by simply changing the sandwich filling. There are many suggestions with which you can experiment.

In the lunchbox menus that follow, I occasionally make recommendations on quantities, but these should be age appropriate and suit your child's individual appetite. The same basic principles apply in terms of the contents for older children. Just increase the quantities accordingly.

The lunchbox is only part of your child's balanced diet, and shouldn't be a substitute for breakfast. For those who rise too early in the morning, or those who just can't face breakfast, a home-made rusk with tea or a fruit smoothie might be the answer. See pages 68–71 for more details.

TIPS

Don't leave the preparation of the lunchbox for the morning before school. There is generally too much happening in the mornings for this to be an inspirational time. Prepare the lunchbox the night before and pop it in the fridge overnight.

Involve your children in preparing their own lunchboxes. Have this book handy to guide them through the principles and start them off by following some of the suggested lunchbox menus. Then encourage them to branch out and try some of the variations. You may soon have the family taking over this chore!

General lunchbox 1

- Ready-to-bake multigrain wholemeal roll spread with chutney/mild mustard/creamed horseradish, lettuce and thinly sliced roast beef.
- Small tub of fruit or plain yoghurt (and a spoon).
- Fruit portion: small containers of dried pears, dried fruit roll shapes or sliced kiwi fruit.
- Water and/or juice.
- **Vegetarian option:** Substitute roast beef with goat's cheese and cucumber.

> ### Did you know?
> Multigrain products, which means that a number of other grains or seeds have been added, are becoming more common on our supermarket shelves. Whole-wheat refers to wheat-based products, wholemeal refers to bread products such as rye and oats.

TIPS

For small mouths, use a flat, soft roll and slice the beef into strips so it's easier to bite and chew.
When buying roast beef, select the fully cooked version and not 'rare' beef, as the rare version may tint the sandwich an off-putting pinkish colour.
Roll the slices of beef before inserting them into the roll.

General lunchbox 2

- Pasta salad (pasta, tinned tuna, chopped tomato, avocado, parsley and mayonnaise in a container – and a spoon).
- 4 x lightly spread wholemeal crispbreads (enclose in wax wrap and then in a plastic zipper-locked bag).
- 2 x sesame breadsticks (broken in half to fit into the lunchbox).
- 1 x cheddar wedge.
- Fruit portion: banana, a small bunch of grapes and/or a hard-fleshed pear.
- Water and/or juice.
- **Vegetarian option:** Substitute tuna with hard-boiled egg or mozzarella chunks, and swap the parsley for fresh basil.

TIP

Whenever you need to include a spoon, wrap it in a colourful paper serviette. Not only does the serviette serve a practical purpose, but it also looks more festive.

Date balls *(page 70)*

Banana smoothie *(page 69)*

Toasted bagel with smoked chicken breasts, mango slices and raspberries *(General lunchbox 7, page 39)*

Melon and Parma ham wraps *(page 59)*

Brown rice salad *(Sports lunchbox 10, page 53)*

Vegetable shapes and crudités *(Vegetarian lunchbox 4, page 42)*

Beetroot salad with onion rings, cheese
and a crusty bread roll (*Vegetarian lunchbox 2, page 41*)

Crispbread with beetroot pâté (*Vegetarian lunchbox 6, page 43*)

General lunchbox 3

- Croissant spread with grainy mustard or mayonnaise, and topped with a few slices of cold ham, fresh lettuce and grated cheddar or sliced mozzarella.
- Raw baby carrots – washed, not peeled.
- Small container with peanuts and seedles raisins or currants.
- Fruit portion: whole apple or sliced watermelon or papaya (when in season) in separate container.
- Water and/or juice.
- **Vegetarian option:** Instead of the ham, spread a thin layer of creamed honey or strawberry preserve with the grated cheese.

TIPS

When including white breads such as a croissant, remember to add fibre by including fresh fruit and vegetables.

Wrap the croissant in wax wrap before inserting it into a plastic sandwich bag to keep fresh.

Creamed honey doesn't seep through the bread as much as traditional-style honey and is less like to crystallize.

When using tomatoes on a sandwich, always remove the seeds and only use the fleshy bit.

General lunchbox 4

- Whole-wheat bread with peanut butter.
- Small container of fruit yoghurt (and a spoon).
- Small container with sliced biltong or dried sausage.
- Cucumber fingers.
- Fruit portion: a small fruit kebab (seasonal) will provide variety and colour – sweet melon (cantaloupe), spanspek, purple grapes and watermelon or strawberries and sliced guavas.
- Water and/or juice.
- **Vegetarian option:** Replace the biltong or dried sausage with bread spread with hummus and topped with sliced tomato (seeded) and sprouts.

TIPS

Peanut butter may be replaced with a suitable protein filling for those with nut allergies. Try thin slices of salami or other suitable cold cuts.

Whatever fruits you choose, try to make the colour combinations interesting!

Did you know?

The Vitamin C content of the humble guava is far greater than that of citrus fruits such as oranges, naartjies, tangerines, clementines or grapefruit.

General lunchbox 5

- Buttered spice bun (hot cross bun).
- Chicken drumstick.
- Rosa tomatoes.
- Raw baby carrots – washed, not peeled.
- Cucumber fingers.
- Fruit portion: small, fresh fruit salad (and a spoon).
- Water and/or juice.
- **Vegetarian option:** Replace the drumstick with the couscous fruit salad (see Vegetarian lunchbox 1 on page 41) and replace the fruit portion with a portion of yoghurt.

 Prepare a few chicken drumsticks, freeze them and defrost when needed. Keep the lunchbox cool by, for example, freezing the drink and packing it with the chicken portion. As a general rule, chicken shouldn't be eaten if it has stood for more than six hours unrefrigerated. For this reason, never 'recycle' food that returns in your child's lunchbox after a day at school.

Did you know?
The raisins in spice buns are an excellent source of iron, which is necessary for healthy red blood cells, as well as concentrated fruit sugars for added energy.

General lunchbox 6

- Hotdog roll (yes, white bread!) with crispy lettuce, bacon and tomato (seeded). Use creamed horseradish instead of butter or margarine.
- Raw baby carrots – washed, not peeled.
- Cucumber fingers.
- Small container with Greek-style yoghurt, honey and nuts (and a spoon).
- Fruit portion: dried-fruit squares.
- Water and/or juice.
- **Vegetarian option:** Replace the bacon with lightly fried Haloumi cheese slices.

 Instead of placing carrots and cucumber in a plastic bag or container, tie them into a bundle with some raffia.

Did you know?
Although whole-wheat bread and rolls are preferable, an occasional slice of white bread is still a perfectly good source of carbohydrate and will provide the bulk and energy your child requires. However, when using white bread, be sure to include fibre-rich additions such as raw carrots, and fruit – fresh or dried. The occasional use of white bread will also add variety to the diet.

General lunchbox 7

- Buttered cheese roll or toasted bagel. Top roll or bagel with smoked chicken breasts, raspberries and a few mango slices. Mix coriander pesto with some mayonnaise or plain yoghurt and use as a dressing. Top with a few sprouts if you like.
- Small bag of home-popped popcorn in an airtight container or zipper-locked plastic bag.
- Fruit portion: apple, banana and a small container with seedless raisins or currants.
- Water and/or juice.
- **Vegetarian option:** Omit the chicken and replace it with a vegetable kebab by stringing the rosa tomatoes, some feta cheese cubes, celery chunks and/or baby corn onto a skewer, separating the items with fresh basil leaves.

Did you know?

Popcorn made in the microwave is a great source of energy and insoluble fibre, but without the oil of conventional popcorn. Be sure to choose a brand without any additives and colorants or preservatives, or at least as little as possible.

General lunchbox 8

- Wholemeal pita bread stuffed with shredded, skinless chicken breasts (smoked, optional) combined with chopped dried apricots, parsley and shredded lettuce. Use a little Greek-style yoghurt to combine the ingredients. Wrap the pita in wax wrap before you put it into a sandwich bag or zipper-locked plastic bag.
- Home-made or suitable commercial oat crunchies.
- Fruit portion: peeled or whole orange, naartjie, tangerine or clementine, or a small bunch of red seedless grapes.
- Water and/or juice.
- **Vegetarian option:** Replace the chicken with grated cheddar cheese, cucumber slices and fresh lettuce. Moisten with some mayonnaise, or crème fraîche.

For easy-to-peel oranges, make incisions at regular intervals along the outer skin from the tip of the orange to the base, taking care to cut only through the peel and not into the flesh. Then make a small round incision at the top of the orange, about 25 mm in diameter. Gently lift the 'lid' off the orange. it's now much easier for little fingers to peel away the segments of the outer peel.

cool lunchboxes

General lunchbox 9

- Whole-wheat seeded roll with ham or turkey, lettuce and grated cheddar cheese.
- Small container with dried peaches.
- Fruit portion: small container with halved fresh strawberries.
- Water and/or juice.
- **Vegetarian option:** Replace the ham or turkey with mashed avocado and lemon juice, topped with sliced, hard-boiled eggs. Season with a grinding of sea salt and black pepper.

TIPS

Use this as an open sandwich for an office lunch. Store the avocado mixture and peeled hard-boiled egg in separate containers, and combine them only when ready to eat. This is also great on rye bread.

Instead of using grated cheese, thinly slice cheese for your sandwich using a potato peeler. The 'peeled' cheese will also change the look of the sandwich to create visual variety.

Did you know?
Avocados are one of nature's most wonderful fruits. Packed with vitamins and minerals, they also contain all the essential amino acids and essential fatty acids the body needs.

General lunchbox 10

- Whole-wheat or rye bread spread with creamed honey, Marmite®, Bovril® or any other favourite spread.
- Mini kebabs with small cubes of tomato (or baby tomatoes), gherkin and cheese wedged together on either side of a portion of rolled turkey, ham, chicken, beef or other cold meat. (Use toothpicks for the kebab, but remember that these are suitable only for children older than 4 years.)
- Raw baby carrots – washed, not peeled.
- Mini rice cakes with yoghurt topping.
- Fruit portion: container of sliced papaw or whatever fruit is in season.
- Water and/or juice.
- **Vegetarian option:** Simply leave out the cold meat, and add a small container with a few roughly chopped cashew nuts.

Did you know?
If your child suffers from indigestion, flatulence or constipation, a regular portion of papaw is an excellent remedy. Papaw contains natural enzymes that help break down food and makes digestion much easier.

cool
lunchboxes

Vegetarian lunchbox menus

Vegetarians are generally separated into two groups. Vegans eat only plant foods and avoid all animal products, including dairy and eggs, while conventional vegetarians may also include dairy products and eggs in their diet.

The latter isn't nearly as restricting as a vegan diet, and there is a multitude of choices that are both nutritious and delicious. Because vegans don't consume eggs or dairy, it's best that they supplement their diet with a good multivitamin and multimineral that contains vitamins D and B12.

The general lunchbox ideas on pages 36–40 all offer vegetarian options, but here are a few more delicious lunchboxes for both children and adults.

Vegetarian lunchbox 1

◆ Couscous with chopped fresh fruit. Use heated apple juice to make the couscous and add a variety of chopped fruit. Include a small container of honeyed yoghurt and a spoon.
◆ Small container with raw almonds or mixed raw nuts.
◆ Water (the juice content is already included in the making of the couscous).
◆ **Vegan option:** Simply omit the yoghurt and honey.

Couscous is processed semolina coated with wheat flour. If you are highly intolerant or sensitive to wheat products, replace the couscous with a few slices of buttered, wheat-free rye bread.

Vegetarian lunchbox 2

◆ Beetroot salad made with fresh, cooked beetroot chopped into chunks and mixed with rocket, steamed green beans or broccoli or green asparagus, or both. Add onion rings or spring onions and top with crumbled goat's cheese or chunky cottage cheese.
◆ Crusty bread roll, buttered.
◆ Fruit portion: dried fruit roll, such as guava or peach.
◆ Water and/or juice.
◆ **Vegan option:** Omit the cheese and add toasted sesame and sunflower seeds.

If the salad isn't going to be eaten straight away, store the cheese separately and add it just before eating. I usually dress this salad with a good drizzle of olive oil and a grinding of black pepper.

Vegetarian lunchbox 3

- Mushroom and green asparagus salad. Marinate white button mushrooms in olive oil, garlic and lemon or lime juice and a dash of wholegrain mustard for about as long as it takes to prepare the asparagus. Steam the asparagus for a minute or two and plunge in ice water. Toss rocket leaves and/or watercress with the asparagus and marinated mushrooms. Add a few strips of red and/or yellow pepper for crunch and visual appeal. Pack a fork.
- Multigrain roll, buttered.
- Wedge of mature cheddar cheese.
- Fruit portion: banana and orange, naartjie, tangerine or clementine.
- Water and/or juice.
- **Vegan option:** Omit the cheese and butter.

Use any leftover mushroom marinade as a salad dressing. You could also use long-stemmed broccoli if asparagus is unavailable.

Prepare a whole batch of marinated mushrooms and store in the refrigerator for up to three days. Add the asparagus and leaves just before use.

Vegetarian lunchbox 4

- Vegetable shapes and crudités.
- Small container with chunky cottage cheese as a dip.
- Sesame breadsticks. (Wrap some parma ham around the tips of the breadsticks for a non-vegetarian option.)
- Fruit portion: pear (sliced, if desired, and eaten with the cottage cheese).
- Water and/or juice.
- **Vegan option:** Omit the cottage cheese. Use hummus as a dip for the crudités.

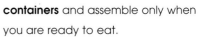

Fresh vegetables cut into bite-sized strips, florets or fingers with a delicious dip is a wonderful way to have a snack meal. **Take traditional crudités one step further** by including cooked, fresh beetroot. Cut the beetroot into thick slices, then cut out shapes using a cookie cutter. If circumstances permit, top the vegetable shapes with cottage cheese and round off with a grinding of black pepper. **Keep the vegetable shapes, crudités and cottage cheese in separate containers** and assemble only when you are ready to eat.

Vegetarian lunchbox 5

- Coleslaw wrap. Make the filling using shredded cabbage or lettuce, grated carrots, toasted sunflower seeds, pecan nuts and a few seedless raisins. Moisten with mayonnaise or Greek-style yoghurt and season to taste. Add strips of yellow and/or red pepper if desired. To assemble, place some filling near the base of the wrap (see Tip). Fold the lower end of the wrap over the filling, then fold the left side halfway across. Fold the right side over to meet the left flap to complete the wrap.
- Fruit portion: a small bunch of grapes.
- Water and/or juice.
- **Vegan option:** Omit the mayonnaise or yoghurt.

Use a naan bread, roti, burrito, tortilla, Lebanese round or cold pancake as a base for the wrap.

Vegetarian lunchbox 6

- Wholemeal crispbread.
- Pâté of choice (and a plastic knife).
- Cocktail gherkins.
- Rosa tomatoes.
- Baby corn.
- Celery sticks.
- Small wedge of gouda cheese.
- Fruit portion: nectarine or another kind of peach.
- Water and/or juice.
- **Vegan option:** Omit the cheese.

TIPS

There are a number of good ready-to-use pâtés on the market. Try the roasted vegetable or mushroom varieties. Decant a portion into a smaller container to be applied when ready to eat.

Wrap the crispbread in clingfilm and be sure to place the vegetable ingredients in a separate plastic bag so that the crispbread doesn't become soft.

Vegetarian lunchbox 7

- Stuffed black mushrooms. Roughly chop a few washed radishes, spring onions, toasted sunflower seeds and sultanas. Mix with chunky cottage cheese and spoon into the hollow of the mushrooms where the stalk has been removed. Finish off with a grinding of black pepper. Add some chopped garlic and parsley to the mixture, if desired.
- A few slices of buttered rye bread.
- Fruit portion: nectarine or another kind of peach.
- Water and/or juice.
- **Vegan option:** Omit the butter and use hummus instead of cottage cheese.

 Use only the freshest, fleshiest mushrooms for this recipe. If you can't find good quality black mushrooms, use Portobello mushrooms instead.

Vegetarian lunchbox 8

- Avocado on rye. Mash a firm, ripe avocado with some lemon juice, salt and pepper and spread a generous amount over the bread. Top with rocket and watercress.
- Fruit portion: a small bunch of black grapes.
- Water and/or juice.

Did you know?

Avocados contain no cholesterol and are rich in disease-fighting antioxidants. They are also high in vitamins A, C and E.

Many of the rye bread products contain a small amount of wheat flour to achieve a lighter, less dense loaf. If you are wheat intolerant, experiment with these varieties and monitor the effects. If highly intolerant, stick to the 100 per cent rye options.

Vegetarian lunchbox 9

- Corn on the cob, cooked and chilled.
- Penne tomato salad. Cook penne until *al denté*, then drain and drizzle with olive oil to prevent the pasta from sticking together. Allow to cool. Meanwhile, chop up a few firm, ripe tomatoes, add sliced raw mushrooms, chopped garlic, olive oil, salt and pepper, and leave to marinate. When the pasta has cooled, pop it into a container and spoon the tomato mixture over the top. If desired, add fresh basil leaves and a crumbling of goat's cheese.
- Fruit portion: banana or apple.
- Water and/or juice.
- **Vegan option:** Simply omit the cheese.

Did you know?

Garlic (raw or cooked) builds the body's immune system. It also reduces high blood pressure and lowers cholesterol in the bloodstream. Garlic also has antibacterial properties.

Vegetarian lunchbox 10

- Egg mayonnaise on high-protein brown bread. Chop hard-boiled eggs and moisten with enough mayonnaise to coat the eggs – don't make it too soggy. Add salt and pepper. You don't need to butter the bread when using a moist filling such as this.
- Fruit portion: chunks of sweet melon and summer melon.
- Water and/or juice.
- **Vegan option:** Substitute the egg and mayonnaise with your favourite pâté.

TIPS

Wrap the sandwich in wax wrap before inserting it into a zipper-locked plastic bag. This will not only help to retain its freshness, but will also prevent the telltale odour associated with boiled egg.

When using strong-smelling ingredients, such as boiled egg or strong cheese, place a large sprig of rosemary in the lunchbox. It looks good when you lift the lid, and imparts the lovely fresh smell associated with this herb.

Sports lunchbox menus

Sports nutrition has become a highly specialized science and has mushroomed into an industry of its own, with many sports enthusiasts devoting their entire career to its development. Optimum performance on the sports field is ultimately determined by the general health of yourself or your child. There are, of course, many books that deal with this topic, so I will focus only on the lunchbox. These lunchboxes have been packed according to a specific formula, but you may adapt the quantities according to your child's needs and level of activity. The gender of your child will also influence quantities.

Protein versus carbohydrates

There is a lot of hype around high-protein diets for athletic or even active children and perhaps this needs to be put into perspective. The body only needs 40–80 grams of protein per day, and the prime function of that protein is to build and restore cells. A secondary function, which protein doesn't perform very efficiently, is to provide energy. Too much protein in the diet will put a strain on the body as it tries to process it all. During protein metabolism, toxic waste products are released and these need to be processed by the kidneys and excreted from the body via urine. But, in ridding itself of these toxins, the body also loses vital minerals such as calcium, potassium and magnesium.

Protein does, however, maintain the blood sugar at reasonable levels for much longer than carbohydrates. Once again, balance is important when it comes to preparing meals for sporting children. The sports lunchbox forms a critical part of providing the system with necessary nutrients and water. The lunch should always include fruit, which provides the quick-release sugars and also contains almost 80 per cent water as well as pectin, which aids digestion. Complex carbohydrates (all vegetables, whole grains, brown rice, peas, beans, lentils, sweet potatoes and potatoes) also provide great snacks for active individuals. These carbohydrates contain complex sugars, which are released at a slower rate than that of fruit, but more importantly, each unit of carbohydrate – in the form of glycogen – is also bound with nine units of water. This water becomes available when the glycogen is converted into energy for the body.

Did you know?

Boys generally go through a growth spurt in their early teens and tend to develop huge appetites at this point. Very often – but not always – the development of their physique coincides with a growing interest in overtly physical sports, such as rugby or soccer, which spurs on the process.

Juice, water and sports drinks

The role of water has already been discussed in detail, as well as some of the downfalls of fruit juice. Here, however, fruit juice has an important role to play. When it comes to sport, natural fruit juice is a very valuable partner. Quick-release sugars must be included in the sports lunchbox and for those who are physically active. Grape juice is a good choice as it boasts one of the fastest releasing sugars. Apple juice – with its relatively slower-releasing sugars – is, on the other hand, also a great choice, especially for the school lunchbox, because the slow release of sugar keeps blood sugar at a reasonable level.

You can use fruit juice specifically to increase energy levels, but don't forget about water. Water is a valuable 'nutrient' in the sporting diet. It is very easy for athletes to dehydrate as thirst sensors are inhibited during performance. It is, therefore, a good idea to hydrate the body by drinking plenty of water before doing any strenuous activity.

To rehydrate the body, drink natural fruit juices such as apple or grape juice, which are good sources of natural glucose without added sugar, preservatives or colorants. No artificial sports drink can match the combination of nutrients in the correct balance that grape or apple juice provide. Unfortunately, many sports drinks contain mostly glucose, a simple sugar that spikes the blood sugar unnecessarily high, and also contain harmful additives and colorants.

Guidelines to sports snacking

- Drink plenty of water before you start – and while you are doing sport, if possible.
- Avoid commercial sports drinks; drink fresh, clear apple or grape juice instead.
- Eat plenty of complex carbohydrates such as whole grains, including whole-wheat bread and brown rice, and raw vegetables.
- Take in simple sugars such as fresh fruit and honey to boost your energy levels.
- Include a portion of protein that is easy to digest, such as tinned tuna or nuts, especially almonds.
- Avoid taking in too much dairy while you are active; this could lead to a build-up of phlegm. Rather keep your dairy portion (small wedge of hard cheese or portion of probiotic yoghurt) for the end of the match or practice.

 A clever way to combine protein with simple sugars is to include honeyed nut brittle (see page 70) in your sports snack.

The sports snack formula

- Water (prevents dehydration).
- Juice (provides hydration and energy).
- Protein in moderation (stabilizes blood-sugar levels).
- Carbohydrate to form the bulk of the snack (provides energy).
- Fresh fruit (hydration and fibre).
- Occasional high-energy treat, such as date balls (see page 70) or honeyed nut brittle (see page 70) for instant energy.

Did you know?

Sunflower seeds are powerful little morsels.

They contain approximately 23 per cent protein, including all the essential amino acids, as well as vitamins E and B complex, magnesium, iron, calcium and fibre.

Pumpkin seeds are exceptionally high in protein, unsaturated fats and Vitamin B complex. They are also a good source of phosphorus, iron and zinc.

Sports lunchbox 1

- Cool, fresh water.
- Apple juice.
- Bow-tie pasta salad. Mix tinned tuna, chopped tomato, onion, yellow pepper, cucumber and fresh parsley into cooked and drained bow-tie (farfalle) pasta. Drizzle with fresh lemon and olive oil. Include a fork.
- Whole-wheat or rye bread, buttered.
- Fruit portion: banana, watermelon or orange.
- Honeyed nut brittle (see page 70) or date balls (see page 70).

 Ring the changes. Use tinned salmon instead of tuna for a more sophisticated flavour.

Did you know?

Onions (raw or cooked) contain a very powerful natural antioxidant. They help prevent cancer, reduce high blood pressure and lower cholesterol in the bloodstream.

Penne tomato salad with mushrooms and olive oil (*Vegetarian lunchbox 9, page 45*)

Mushroom and green asparagus salad
(Vegetarian lunchbox 3, page 42)

Mini kebabs of tomato, gherkin, cheese and cold meat (*General lunchbox 10, page 40*)

Mini meatball and tomato kebabs *(Sports lunchbox 5, page 50)*

Bunny chow *(Sports lunchbox 8, page 52)*

Stuffed black mushrooms served with rye bread
(Vegetarian lunchbox 7, page 44)

Lamb and tzatziki on slices of rye bread *(page 63)*

Spaghetti Genovese with a sprinkle of goat's cheese *(Sports lunchbox 3, page 49)*

Sports lunchbox 2

- Cool, fresh water.
- Grape juice.
- Potato salad pita pocket. Boil unpeeled and halved baby potatoes until soft, then combine them with mayonnaise, chopped spring onions, hard-boiled egg, crispy bacon bits and crumbled feta cheese. Season to taste, and add some watercress and alfalfa sprouts if desired. Fill the pita pocket and wrap up in wax wrap and then in foil to keep the filling in place and the contents fresh.
- Fruit portion: naartjie, tangerine or clementine.
- Raisins.
- **Vegetarian option:** Simply omit the bacon.

 If the pita pocket is too filling for younger children, simply pop the potato salad in a small container and provide a fork.

Sports lunchbox 3

- Cool, fresh water.
- Mango juice.
- Spaghetti Genovese. Place halved baby potatoes into salted boiling water and cook for 5 minutes. Add halved green beans to the same pot. Cook for 5 minutes, before adding the spaghetti. Cook until the spaghetti is *al dente*. Drain and add a few glugs of olive oil, then stir in some basil pesto and leave to cool. Spoon into a suitable container and crumble some goat's cheese over the top for added protein and flavour.
- Fruit portion: naartjie, tangerine, clementine, apple, pear, or whatever is in season.

 To make the spaghetti easier to eat, break the strands into finger lengths before cooking.

Did you know?

Pasta and potatoes are both complex carbohydrates, but the addition of pesto and cheese provides valuable protein, thus making this meal well suited to active, sporting children.

This is also a great supper option, so if you don't have time to eat it before or after your sporting activity, warm it up at home and have it for dinner.

Sports lunchbox 4

- Cool, fresh water.
- Apple juice.
- Double-decker BLT. Use three slices of whole-wheat bread to make this sandwich. Butter each slice and spread with creamed horseradish. Top the first slice with butter lettuce and sliced tomato (seeded), then place the second slice of bread on top. Spread with horseradish and sprinkle over a generous helping of crispy bacon bits. Cover with the third slice of bread. Secure with toothpicks, slice in half and wrap firmly in clingfilm.

It is not a good idea to use toothpicks for younger children. Rather assemble all the ingredients onto a soft roll and wrap in clingfilm.

Did you know?
Mangoes are powerful multinutrient fruits containing many vitamins and minerals that the body needs, including very important antioxidants.

- Fruit portion: sliced watermelon or mango.

Sports lunchbox 5

- Cool, fresh water.
- Mango or apple juice.
- Mini meatball and tomato kebabs. Thread mini meatballs, rosa tomatoes, cocktail gherkins and basil leaves onto skewers.
- Sliced whole-wheat bread, buttered.
- Fruit portion: naartjie, tangerine, clementine, apple, pear or whatever is in season.
- **Vegetarian option:** Substitute the meatballs with cubes of mozzarella.

There are some delicious, ready-to-eat meatballs available from delis and supermarkets. If you prefer, ask your butcher to prepare some lean beef mince and make your own. For a basic meatball recipe, see page 71.

cool
lunchboxes

Sports lunchbox 6

- Cool, fresh water.
- Orange juice.
- Beef biltong sandwich. Spread a lavish amount of cream cheese over one slice of bread – use a flavoured cream cheese if preferred. Sprinkle over some alfalfa sprouts. Spread another slice of bread with sweet chilli sauce and sandwich together with the first slice. Spread the outside of the sandwich with a thin layer of cream cheese and coat generously with biltong shavings. Wrap the sandwich in wax wrap before placing it in a plastic sandwich bag.
- Fruit portion: apple, or whatever is in season.

 The biltong sandwich works best on soft brown bread and even white bread. To make it easier to eat, cut the sandwich into smaller portions before coating with biltong. And don't restrict this to sports lunches – it makes for a great office snack too.

Sports lunchbox 7

- Cool, fresh water.
- Apple juice.
- Mini chicken kebabs. Thread bite-sized portions of cooked or smoked chicken, cucumber and pineapple onto skewers or toothpicks.
- Sliced pumpernickel or pumpkin-seed bread, buttered.
- Fruit portion: a small container with chunks of green melon and some black grapes (and a fork).
- Honeyed nut brittle (see page 70).

 For older kids, pop a toothpick instead of a fork into the container to use for eating the melon chunks.

Sports lunchbox 8

- Cool, fresh water.
- Grape juice.
- Bunny chow. Using a soft roll, cut a 'lid' on one side and scoop out some of the bread to make a cavity. Fill this cavity with mild curried mince or leftover bobotie. Add a dollop of fruit chutney and some chopped fresh coriander, and put the 'lid' back on. Wrap securely with wax wrap and string, then wrap again in foil.
- Fruit portion: naartjie, tangerine, clementine, apple, pear, or whatever is in season.
- Date balls (see page 70).
- **Vegetarian option:** Use soya mince for the curry or bobotie.

 This rather substantial meal can be heated if the facilities are available, but is equally good eaten cold.

Sports lunchbox 9

- Cool, fresh water.
- Apple juice.
- Salami on rye. Butter slices of fresh rye bread and top with lettuce, cucumber and thin slices of salami. Spread the top slice of bread with a thin layer of whole-grain mustard, creamed horseradish or mayonnaise. Wrap in wax wrap and place into a plastic sandwich bag.
- Fruit portion: a bunch of grapes, or whatever is in season.
- **Vegetarian option:** Replace the salami with smoked mozzarella or cheddar cheese.

Did you know?

Cucumbers consist of around 95 per cent water, and are also a source of Vitamin C and fibre.

Salami has been used in Italian cooking for centuries. The fat used in the production of salami is always derived from pork.

 Avoid salami if you have a cholesterol problem. Replace it with shaved turkey breast or smoked chicken.

Sports lunchbox 10

- Cool, fresh water.
- Grape juice.
- Brown rice salad. Combine chopped tomato, onion or spring onion, garlic, cucumber, avocado chunks, sunflower seeds and diced mozzarella cheese. Squeeze fresh lemon juice over, taking care to coat the avocado to prevent discoloration. Add cooked and cooled brown rice to the above mixture, along with some chopped fresh herbs, such as parsley, basil or coriander, or be daring and use some of each. Drizzle with good quality olive oil to moisten.
- Fruit portion: apple or pear, or whatever is in season.
- Banana muffin.

TIPS

Use whole-wheat pasta instead of brown rice, if preferred.
Use the same salad ingredients, but make it taste and look different by using the tri-coloured 'screw' pasta.
For meat-eaters, simply add strips of cooked or smoked chicken or turkey.

Sports lunchbox 11

- Cool, fresh water.
- Apple juice.
- Salmon croissant. Mash avocado with enough lemon juice to prevent discoloration, and season to taste. Spread thickly on the base of the croissant. Top with flakes of tinned salmon and chopped fresh chives, gherkins or even capers for a more sophisticated flavour. Wrap in wax wrap before placing into a sandwhich bag.
- Cucumber fingers.
- Fruit portion: watermelon wedges.

> **Did you know?**
> **Tinned salmon has a much more delicate flavour and texture than that of tinned tuna** and makes a nice variation to this lunchbox. An added advantage is that the salmon provides important omega 3 oils.
> **The cucumber and watermelon increase the water and fibre content** of this lunchbox.

Snacking en route

In the car

My mother spoilt us rotten when it came to food. Leaving to go on holiday, we could hardly wait for the car to pull out of the garage before asking what she had packed for us to nibble! Now my own children are much the same. In my mother's defence, of course, there weren't as many food options then as we have today when we travel long distances. Nowadays, it's much easier, especially since modern filling stations began to dot the countryside, and you are never too far from somewhere to stock up or grab a quick meal. In my experience, however, it's better to have a couple of nibbles handy to keep the blood sugar constant. The last thing you need on a long car journey is a bunch of kids with either low blood sugar or a hyperactive car load as a result of too much fast food, sweets and fizzy drinks! But don't be too fussy. Keep the menu simple and exclude obvious items, such as biltong and dried sausage, which will make everyone thirsty and the driver will have to endure endless pit stops that are inevitable when the passengers have had too much to drink. Speaking of drinking… Try to get your family to drink only water. Fill easy-drinking containers (like the ones cyclists use) with ice and cold water. Nothing refreshes like cool water.

Fresh fruit is also a great option – especially the old favourites, such as apples, bananas, pears and naartjies, tangerines or clementines – but remember to take a packet for all the peels and waste. And never leave the house without something with which to wipe sticky little fingers!

Potato crisps are often a popular option, but it's best to avoid these. They are packed with colorants and flavourants (MSG), which aren't conducive to a long journey in the car. And, of course, they also make you thirsty. Sandwiches remain the best meal-time solution. They are easy to manage and easy to make – and you could even cater to everyone's personal favourites without too much fuss. Wrap each sandwich separately, so each person can enjoy his or hers when hungry. Small muffins are also a great treat and easy to eat.

Some children and even adults are prone to motion (car) sickness. Avoid fatty foods and encourage them to eat an apple or a dry water biscuit.

A great treat for my children is the sugar-free gum I allow them to chew after the meal. The chewing helps stimulate the production of saliva, which in turn helps cleanse the mouth and teeth. Chewing gum also keeps the mouth occupied, and less likely to require constant feeding!

Day hiking

I wasn't born into hiking – I married into it! I married into a family that takes their hiking very seriously and I am a proud daughter-in-law of a granny who celebrated her 50-year anniversary as an active member of the Cape Town Mountain Club. This year she celebrated her 77th birthday, and can still outpace me! Along the way, I have picked up a few valuable tips. The most important lesson is that simplicity is key!

- Always prepare a flask of tea. We prefer rooibos tea, which seems to retain its flavour better than Ceylon tea, but keep the milk in a separate container.
- Raisins. Fresh fruit is just too heavy and cumbersome to carry.
- Date balls (see page 70). Pack these into a slim container with a secure lid, so that they aren't squashed in the backpack.
- Tammy's rusks (see page 68). Rusks are such a winner – not only do they fill the gaps, but they are also light and easy to carry and are great when dipped into hot tea.

- Ginger biscuits. The hard commercial varieties are quite resilient and survive even the bumpy ride in a backpack.
- Dark chocolate. Yes, it works! Milk chocolate, however, doesn't – partly because it melts quicker than dark chocolate, and partly because it's much sweeter than dark chocolate and induces thirst.

We always carry water, even if it's just a short stroll. You just never know when you might need it. If we are due to stay out for the day, we also pack a small portable cooker and a jaffle iron (pie iron) that transforms ready-made cheese sandwiches into welcome toasted treats, especially when you are tired and weary and the icy mountain wind is turning your cheeks into little red apples! Another essential item is, of course, a wet cloth to wipe sticky hands and faces – so keep it lean, keep it mean, and don't forget the water!

officebound &
outbound

Get sophisticated!

The ingredients for office lunches and picnics are a little more sophisticated than those of school lunchboxes, and can even be adventurous, but most still make use of easily accessible ingredients. They can also be readily substituted if they happen to be unavailable. Make sure you stock your 'clever cupboard' with a few of the basic suggestions listed on page 32. This way, you will be able to whip up a delectable picnic or office lunch that will be the envy of your colleagues and fellow picnickers. In this chapter, I have offered suggestions for the main part of the meal, which you can mix and match to suit your mood and the occasion.

General tips

If you go to the trouble of packing a good lunch, remember to include the little things that make the effort worthwhile:

- Always have salt and pepper to hand (use grinders, if possible). Keep a set in the office kitchen or in your picnic basket.
- Pack the fillings separately and assemble your sandwiches at the last minute.
- Keep salad dressings separate and add only at the last minute.
- Colourful napkins add a festive touch, and cloth napkins add a touch of elegance to any setting.
- Include a knife, fork or spoon as necessary.
- A few sprigs of fresh herbs make for a fragrant garnish.
- If transporting cheese, wrap each cheese separately in wax paper or plastic and place a large sprig of rosemary in the container to mask the cheesy odour when the container is opened.

Ideas with fruit

Fresh mango and Greek yoghurt

Top slices of fresh mango with Greek-style or fat-free natural yoghurt, and drizzle with honey.

Sprinkle toasted pine kernels or sunflower seeds over the top of the mango and yoghurt for added energy.

Did you know?

Mangoes are one of the best sources of vitamins, minerals and trace elements.

They are also a good source of fibre.

Nectarine salad

Squeeze some lime juice over slices of nectarines and a handful of raspberries, and tear in a few mint leaves. Drizzle with honey if additional sweetness is required. Greek-style or fat-free natural yoghurt is also a great accompaniment to this salad.

You could serve the nectarine salad as a dessert, or on a toasted waffle or flapjack for a more substantial snack. It's also great as a mid-morning 'pick-me-up'. **Replace the nectarines with fresh plums** and omit the lemon juice.

Melon and Parma ham wraps

Melon and Parma ham is an old favourite, but it's still a winner. Wrap thin slices of Parma or prosciutto around wedges of melon, or substitute firm, ripe nectarines for the melon.

Fruit kebabs

Fruit kebabs are a great way to portion fruit and I often include them in the school lunchbox. And it's a great snack for the office and even for picnics. They are easy to eat, look really appetising and you don't get your fingers sticky. The art, however, is in the selection of fruits, which need to complement each other. Cut the fruit into bite-sized chunks and string these onto a skewer or toothpick, alternating the colours and textures. Try these combinations:

FRUIT KEBAB 1

papaw (or guava)

banana

pear

orange

strawberry

 Drizzle the pulp of a granadilla across the kebab, taking special care to drizzle some over the banana. This will help prevent discoloration and add an extra dimension to your fruit salad.

FRUIT KEBAB 2

guava

strawberry

small papaya

kiwi fruit

sweet melon

FRUIT KEBAB 3

watermelon

mint leaves

black grapes

Intersperse the fruit with the mint leaves.

FRUIT KEBAB 4

banana

strawberry

lime or lemon juice (to prevent discoloration)

Sandwich the strawberries between chunks of banana and squeeze the lime or lemon juice over.

Healthy, hearty salads

Most of the following suggestions are suitable for vegetarians and are low in cholesterol. Although they are based on a high complex carbohydrate, the combination of ingredients makes them a fairly substantial meal without being fattening. Some variations contain animal protein, but these may be omitted or substituted if desired.

Leafy salads generally don't lend themselves to packed lunches, as they tend to wilt or dry out, but what does work very well are rocket leaves or watercress. These are pungent leaves and add great value to any meal. If salad leaves are required, wash thoroughly and pat dry before placing them in an airtight container.

What makes great lunch salads is a base of cooked pasta (conventional wheat or 100 per cent buckwheat), couscous, brown rice or rice noodles. These salads tolerate dressings very well, and are substantial meals in their own right. They are also a good disguise for leftovers!

Did you know?
Brown rice is a very important source of vitamins B1 (thiamine) and B2 (riboflavin), which are necessary for energy metabolism. Brown rice is also very high in natural fibre and is excellent for the weight conscious with the bonus that it doesn't skimp on nutrition!

Basic brown rice salad

Toss together cooked and cooled brown rice, and chopped tomatoes, cucumber, spring onion and a generous amount of shredded fresh parsley, basil and coriander. Add a squeeze of lemon. (A dash of balsamic vinegar will add a Mediterranean flavour!)

Use the basic brown rice as a base and add the following ingredients for a pleasant change:

- Avocado and sliced button mushrooms, sprinkled with fresh lime/lemon juice.
- Chargrilled courgettes (baby marrows) and red and yellow peppers.
- Cooked lentils (to add texture).

The above-mentioned ingredients are suitable for those who are lactose or wheat intolerant, cholesterol sufferers, and vegans.

- Fresh pineapple chunks and slivers of ham.
- Fresh whole basil leaves and feta or mozzarella.

These simple ingredients are given a real lift by the fresh herbs. Be generous with the herbs. Not only do they add great flavour to the salad, but they are also packed with vitamins and minerals.

Honeyed nut brittle *(page 70)*

Multigrain wholemeal roll with roast beef and lettuce *(General lunchbox 1, page 36)*

Croissant with salmon and avocado (*Sports lunchbox 11, page 53*)

Crispy roll with tomato, mozzarella and basil *(page 62)*

Pasta salads

Use pasta rice or a 'fork-friendly' pasta such as fusilli (screws), farfalle (bow ties) or penne (tubes) as a base, and then vary the ingredients.

- Roasted vegetables and goat's cheese.
- Tinned tuna or salmon with finely chopped gherkins and/or onions.
- Roasted butternut with chunks of feta cheese.
- Strips of rare roast beef with plenty of fresh chopped coriander, and a sprinkling of lime juice as the dressing.
- Steamed asparagus, toasted pine nuts and sliced boiled eggs, with basil pesto diluted with extra-virgin olive oil and lemon juice as the dressing.
- Chopped fleshy tomatoes that have been marinated in olive oil, chopped garlic and black pepper, and finished with a few fresh basil leaves.

TIPS

Pasta salads can be warmed in winter if heating facilities are available. Most of the ingredients lend themselves to being heated. For example, the roasted vegetables with goat's cheese and the butternut with feta suggestions are both equally delicious served hot or cold. **Shavings of Parmesan add a sense of luxury** to any pasta salad.

Chicken salad

This salad can be used as it is, served with wholewheat bread or crusty rolls, or it can be combined with cooked pasta for a more substantial meal.

Toss together cooked chunks of chicken, chopped spring onions and mango pieces. Add a few pecan nuts and chopped fresh coriander to taste. Drizzle with some good quality olive oil and a squeeze of lemon or lime juice. Season with salt and a grinding of pepper.

Did you know?

Olive oil contains natural antioxidants, which reduce the risk of breast cancer. Olive oil also reduces blood pressure and regulates blood-sugar levels.

Sandwiches and fillings

Be inventive. Make some delicious fillings and then pack them in separate containers. Butter sliced bread or rolls and wrap them in wax paper. When you are ready to eat, simply pile on the filling that you have prepared, grind some fresh black pepper over the top, and you will be the envy of all. Remember to pack a spoon, knife or fork in order to dish up the filling.

Tomato, mozzarella and fresh herbs

Slice crispy rolls or whole-wheat bread, butter them and add slices of seeded plum tomatoes and mozzarella. Add salt and a good grinding of black pepper. Top with torn, fresh basil leaves.

A great variety of tomatoes are available in our supermarkets today. If you can get hold of them, Italian plum (Roma) tomatoes – sometimes referred to as jam tomatoes – are the best choice for lunchboxes. These tomatoes are very fleshy, with very few seeds. They also have a good shelf life if stored in the refrigerator.

Roasted red pepper and feta

Halve a fresh sesame or multigrain roll. Add roasted red peppers and sliced or crumbled feta. Top with a dollop of basil pesto and a few rocket leaves.

Grilled or roasted vegetables

Use any selection of roasted vegetables that have been cooled to room temperature. When ready to eat, pile high onto sliced ciabatta rolls. Add a few strips of raw red onion, if preferred. Top with a grinding of black pepper.

For extra flavour, spread a thick layer of ricotta or cream cheese on the base before piling on the roasted veggies, or top the vegetables with goat's cheese. Add freshly chopped herbs (parsley, chives or basil) for flavour and nutrient value.

officebound & outbound

Lamb and tzatziki

Spread buttered slices of rye bread with tzatziki, and top with leafy lettuce and thin slices of cold roast lamb. Season with a grinding of black pepper and salt as desired.

Cholesterol sufferers may use margarine if they prefer, and should cut away visible fat from the lamb. Make your own low-fat tzatziki by using low-fat yoghurt rather than Greek-style yoghurt, and mixing it with drained and grated cucumber, finely chopped garlic (don't be shy), a dash of lemon juice, and salt and pepper to taste.

Did you know?

Cucumber is a natural diuretic and thus prevents the unwanted build-up of fluid in the body.

Chicken and celery pockets

Shred cooked, skinless chicken breasts and combine with finely diced celery, some cracked walnuts and a few spoons of mayonnaise to form a moist filling. Season with salt and pepper. Spoon the mixture into wholemeal pita pockets.

Keep the chicken and celery filling separate until you are ready to eat the pita. This way, the pita won't become soggy. Roughly chopped parsley sprinkled on top of the filling lends great colour and crunch to the meal, and also provides important vitamins A and C. **For cholesterol sufferers, skinless chicken breasts are a good form of animal protein** and should thus be a regular feature in the diet. For variation, use smoked chicken breasts, or even turkey breasts.

Sausage and mustard roll

The guys will just love this one, but it's not for choles-terol sufferers! Cut and butter long bread rolls, such as hotdog rolls or mini baguettes, and spread with whole-grain Dijon mustard mixed with a little mayonnaise. Add slices of plum tomato and season with salt and pepper. Top with a grilled or fried sausage – cold pork sausages, or bangers, for example, make for a delicious sandwich.

Plum tomatoes are more fleshy and, if seeded, can be used on a sandwich with great success.

If you slice the sausage lengthwise so that it lies flat, the roll will be much easier to eat.

Dijon mustard can be replaced with fruit chutney or creamed horseradish.

Thai chicken wrap

Stir-fry thin strips of chicken breasts in a little hot oil (preferably sesame seed or peanut oil), adding strips of yellow and red peppers, garlic, onion, cour-gettes (baby marrows) and a generous helping of sesame seeds. Toss until the chicken is just cooked and the veggies are still crisp. Sprinkle with soy sauce and stir in some peanut butter. Allow to cool, then refrigerate until required. To assemble, place some filling and torn fresh coriander near the base of the wrap (naan bread, roti, burrito, tortilla, Lebanese round or cold pancake). Fold the lower end of the wrap over the filling, then fold the left side halfway across. Fold the right side over to meet the left flap to complete the wrap.

As an alternative to the chicken stir-fry, use leftover beef stroganoff. Cut the meat into very thin strips and add chopped spring onion and parsley. Add a generous helping of grainy mustard to some sour cream and use as a dressing.

Make the filling the night before, or make extra when you use this as a quick supper dish.

Lettuce wrap

Use butter lettuce to make this wrap. Wash the lettuce and pat dry. Take each leaf and place a slice of rare roast beef and a spoonful of creamed horseradish in the centre. Roll the leaf loosely in its natural direction and secure with a toothpick or, for a more attractive finish, use a wilted garlic chive and tie like a 'parcel'. As an optional extra, add a few chopped gherkins to complement the flavours.

TIPS

As an alternative, use thin slices of smoked salmon instead of the roast beef.
This wrap is best served with buttered rye bread or whole-wheat bread. Sandwich the buttered slices, facing each other, and wrap in clingfilm or foil to keep fresh.
Instead of the gherkins, cucumber matchsticks may be used.
Butter lettuce is quite delicate, so take due care when assembling the wrap.

Quick-and-easy gourmet fillings

Be a little adventurous and try some of the following quick-and-easy gourmet fillings on sandwich bread or in pitas or wraps – or even as toppings on open sandwiches.

- Bocconcini (baby mozzarella), basil leaves and tomato – and add drained anchovy fillets for an extra dimension.
- Prosciutto with oven-roasted vine tomatoes and parmesan shavings.
- Cream cheese, smoked salmon and chopped chives or spring onions – add a squeeze of fresh lemon and chopped fresh dill.
- Smoked chicken, avocado and cranberry sauce.
- Smoked chicken or turkey with butter lettuce, brie and avocado.
- Crispy bacon, blue cheese and chilli jam.
- Roasted vegetables with chilli jam and gorgonzola.

TIPS

Mash avocado with some lemon juice, salt and a grinding of pepper and use it instead of butter or margarine.
These toppings are also great on rice cakes or wheat-free rye bread, for those with wheat intolerance.
To retain freshness, place the fillings in separate containers and only assemble just before eating.

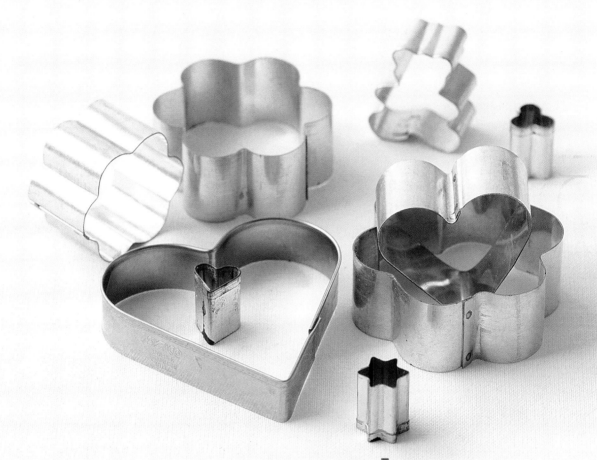

recipes
on the run

Get going!

The recipes on the following pages have been selected to assist people who simply can't face breakfast first thing in the morning, or who have to leave too early and don't have the time to prepare breakfast. The important thing to remember is that we need to 'wake up' our metabolism in the morning by feeding it breakfast. These meal suggestions are transportable and can be munched in the car or sipped on the way to school or work.

Breakfast

YUMMY BREAKFAST MUESLI

500 g butter

1½ cups (300 g) honey

1 packet (100 g) raw almonds, roughly chopped

1 packet (100 g) raw pecan nuts, roughly chopped

1 packet (100 g) raw cashew nuts, roughly chopped

1 packet (100 g) raw walnuts, roughly chopped

4 cups (320 g) oats

2 cups (100 g) puffed wheat

1 cup (30 g) digestive bran

2 cups (240 g) sesame seeds

2 cups (240 g) sunflower seeds

2 cups (160 g) desiccated coconut

1 cup (120 g) poppy seeds

2 cups (90 g) each All-Bran® Hi-Bulk Bran® (optional)

1. Melt the butter and honey.
2. Mix the remaining ingredients in a very large mixing bowl, then make a well in the middle.
3. Add half the butter and honey mixture and mix well, then add the remaining half and mix.
4. Spread the mixture on baking sheets and bake at 180 °C (350 °F; gas mark 4) for 15–20 minutes until golden. Stir occasionally to ensure even browning.
5. Cool and store in airtight containers. To prevent the nuts from going rancid, spoon half the batch into zipper-locked plastic bags and freeze.
6. For sufferers of nut allergies, simply omit the nuts.

TAMMY'S RUSKS

500 g butter or margarine

2 cups (500 ml) milk

2 eggs, beaten

6 cups (720 g) cake flour

4 cups (120 g) digestive bran

1½ cups (300 g) brown sugar

4 tbsp (60 ml) baking powder

1 tsp (5 ml) salt

1. Melt the butter and milk over medium heat, then remove and set aside.
2. Add the eggs to the milk mixture.
3. Mix all the dry ingredients together in a large mixing bowl, and make a well in the centre.
4. Add the milk mixture and stir very well (in one direction only) until 'threads' begin to appear in the dough.
5. Scrape the mixture into a greased oven pan and bake at 180 °C (350 °F; gas mark 4) for approximately 1 hour (test after 45 minutes by inserting a knife into the centre; if it comes out clean, the rusks are done).
6. Remove from the oven and leave to cool.
7. Once completely cold, cut into thin fingers.
8. Place on baking sheets and dry out overnight in a cool oven at 70–100 °C (200 °F; gas mark ¼).
9. Store in airtight containers.

recipes
on the run

Smoothies

Smoothies are a great way to give you and your children's day a kick-start, especially if breakfast isn't your favourite meal. Experiment with different ingredients, and take special note of your children's favourites, then encourage them to make it themselves. Invest in a mug or tumbler with a lid so it can be used in the car if necessary.

For those suffering from lactose (dairy) intolerance, replace the cow's milk with soya milk and/or natural fruit juice.

Strawberry and mango smoothie

Process the flesh of a mango with a few strawberries and a glass of milk. Sometimes, I halve the quantity of milk and replace the other half with vanilla-flavoured yoghurt. Quite delicious!

Mixed berry smoothie

Combine milk and strawberries or other mixed berries to whip up a pink and powerful drink. If you have run out of fresh fruit, you can use frozen berries instead.

Banana smoothie

Process one banana, half a glass of milk and half a glass of Greek-style yoghurt, adding a dollop of honey if more sweetness is required. Pour into a plastic mug and enjoy in the car on the way to school or the office.

Bananas are great for making smoothies. They combine well with a variety of different fruits. Try banana and mango, banana and papaw, or banana with soft, ripe pears. For a slightly sweeter taste, use vanilla-flavoured yoghurt instead of the Greek-style yoghurt.

Did you know?

Bananas are high in vitamins and especially high in potassium and natural sugars.

Quick snacks

These fall under the list of treats, so try not to use them too often as they will lose their 'treat' status. The recipe for date balls is my adaptation of Mary-Ann Shearer's original. The recipe for two-week muffins was given to me by a friend. This recipe was all the rage a few years ago, but my own version is really delicious. These muffins do not rise much, making them ideal for lunchboxes.

DATE BALLS

2 cups (160 g) desiccated coconut
3 cups (450 g) fresh dates, pitted
zest of 1 lemon
3 tbsp (45 ml) orange juice (with fruit cells) or water

1. Using a food processor, pulse the coconut, dates and lemon zest with just enough orange juice or water to make a rough mixture.
2. Pinch off bits of the mixture and roll between your palms to make small balls. Then roll the balls in extra coconut.
3. Refrigerate in an airtight container.
4. For stacking, place a sheet of wax paper between layers of date balls.

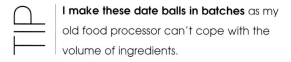 **I make these date balls in batches** as my old food processor can't cope with the volume of ingredients.

HONEYED NUT BRITTLE

2 tbsp (30 ml) butter
½ cup (125 g) honey
1 cup (100 g) whole mixed nuts
3 tbsp (45 ml) sesame seeds (optional)

1. Melt the butter and honey in a saucepan and boil for approximately 15 minutes on medium heat, or until the honey turns a darker brown.
2. Remove from the heat and add the nuts and sesame seeds, stirring to coat them thoroughly.
3. Spread the mixture on a baking sheet and leave to cool.
4. When cool, break into pieces and store in airtight containers, or freeze in zipper-locked plastic bags.

 To speed up the cooling process, pop the baking sheet into the fridge for a few minutes.

recipes
on the run

TWO-WEEK MUFFINS

3 eggs

2 cups (500 ml) milk

1½ cups (375 ml) oil

3 tbsp (45 ml) honey

4 cups (480 g) cake flour

4 tsp (20 ml) bicarbonate of soda

4 tsp (20 ml) baking powder

2 tsp (10 ml) salt

1½ cups (300 g) brown sugar

4 cups (180 g) All-Bran® flakes

1 cup (150 g) seedless raisins

1 cup (100 g) mixed nuts, chopped

1. Beat the eggs, milk, oil and honey together.
2. Sift the flour, bicarbonate of soda, baking powder and salt, and add the rest of the dry ingredients.
3. Make a well in the centre of the dry ingredients, and pour the egg and milk mixture into the well. Stir gently (you don't want to develop the gluten that will make the muffins chewy!) until just mixed.
4. Transfer to an airtight container and refrigerate. Be sure to use within two weeks.
5. When needed, gently turn the mixture with a large metal spoon, and spoon out into greased muffin pans or paper muffin cases.
6. Bake in a preheated oven at 180 °C (350 °F; gas mark 4) for 20 minutes (or 30 minutes if using a giant muffin pan).
7. Simply omit the nuts if allergic.

MINI MEATBALLS

500 g lean beef mince

1 tsp (5 ml) salt

1 tsp (5 ml) ground cloves

½ tsp (2 ml) ground coriander

½ cup (15 g) chopped parsley

1 egg

black pepper

3 tbsp (45 ml) fruit chutney (optional)

1. Mix together the mince, salt, cloves, coriander, parsley and egg.
2. Grind in black pepper to taste, and add fruit chutney if desired.
3. Roll the mince mixture into small balls.
4. Shallow fry or grill for 5–6 minutes until golden brown, or oven bake at 180 °C (350 °F; gas mark 4) for 20 minutes until golden brown and cooked.
5. Allow to cool, then refrigerate until needed.

index